Amiett Kumar is a renowned Law of Attraction and Manifestation coach with nineteen years of experience in manifestation and mindset transformation. Founder of the Readers Books Club, which has over 3 million subscribers, and his own channel, Dr Amiett Kumar, which has over 1 million subscribers, his journey from IT head to global influencer has inspired millions, turning knowledge into a powerful movement of self-growth.

Manifest anything in 100 days

AMIETT KUMAR

EBURY
PRESS

An imprint of Penguin Random House

EBURY PRESS

Ebury Press is an imprint of the Penguin Random House group of companies whose addresses can be found at global.penguinrandomhouse.com

Published by Penguin Random House India Pvt. Ltd
4th Floor, Capital Tower 1, MG Road,
Gurugram 122 002, Haryana, India

First published in Ebury Press by Penguin Random House India 2026

ISBN 9780143477266

Typeset in Adobe Garamond Pro by Manipal Technologies Limited, Manipal
Printed at Thomson Press India Private Limited

www.penguin.co.in

Before You Begin

The Key to Unlocking This Book's Magic

Welcome to your 100-day transformation! But before we begin, let's set some ground rules—because this isn't just a book; it's an experience.

1. *One Chapter. One Day.*
    Read only one chapter per day and absorb it fully. No rushing ahead.
2. *Miss a Day? Start Over.*
    This is your commitment to yourself. If you miss a day, you restart from Day 1. This journey is about discipline and consistency.
3. *Tasks = Transformation.*
    Throughout this book, you will come across interactive exercises—these aren't suggestions; they are part of your manifestation process. Use a pencil to complete each one when you reach it.

4. *Create Your Manifestation Space.*
   I will often ask you to sit in a comfortable position, preferably at a table or a quiet place. Choose this spot right now—this will be your dedicated manifestation zone for the next 100 days.

5. Let's Play a Game!
   Whenever I type 'HI!', you say 'HELLOOO!' out loud.
   Let's try it now—HI! → (**Your turn: HELLOOO!**)

6. *Few Days End with Action.*
   On some days, we will conclude with a task. Manifestation isn't just about thinking; it's about doing. Follow through with every task given.

Are you ready? Let's get started.

Preface

The Law of Attraction, Visualization, Manifestation— when you hear these words, what comes to your mind?

What if I tell you that these concepts can *turn your dreams into reality or shape your life the way you want?*

In one of his interviews with Graham Bensinger, **Virat Kohli** mentioned that three months before a match, he would visualize himself overcoming the best bowler of the opposing team. He spent countless hours in the gym seeing this moment so vividly in his mind that what started as just a thought eventually played out exactly as he had imagined on the field.

So, the question arises:

Does this concept actually work?

Well, why don't you find out for yourself?

How? you ask.

What if I told you that in the next 100 days, you could rewire your mind, attract abundance and manifest the life you've always dreamed of? This book isn't just about theory—it's a step-by-step, action-packed journey into the Law of Attraction like never before. From ancient wisdom to modern science, from mindset shifts to practical techniques, every page is designed to unlock your hidden potential. No fluff, no vague promises— just real transformation. This is not just a book—it's a **100-day challenge** designed specifically for you, the reader, the dreamer, the manifester.

In today's world, the idea of turning dreams into reality has become an abstract concept—something we believe in but struggle to define, a vision without a road map, a goal without a clear strategy. We hear about success stories, but we rarely see a structured path to create our own. You, me and countless others often struggle to take that first step towards our destiny. And even if we do know the next step, we sometimes lack the motivation, discipline or belief to take action.

But I am here to tell you—*this works*.

I have been exactly where you are. I have had dreams that felt distant, goals that seemed too big, and doubts that whispered:

What if this isn't possible?
What if I fail?
What will people think if I can't do it?

But through this journey, I have learnt one powerful truth:

What you dream, you can achieve.

How? You will ask again.

Over the next 100 days, I am not just going to teach you about the Law of Attraction—I am going to guide you step by step, day by day, into applying it in your life. This book is not about passively reading concepts; it's about experiencing the transformation in real time.

All I ask from you is commitment. Just ten to fifteen minutes a day. That's it.

Because if you give these 100 days your full dedication, I promise you—you will see your own Virat Kohli moment.

So, are you ready?

Turn the page. Let's begin our journey of manifestation!

Day 1

Ready, Set, Go!

Before we begin this journey of the *Law of Attraction*, let's first get ready. Think of this like packing your bag before a trip.

The first step to using the Law of Attraction is to first understand it. So, before you move ahead, I want you to sit in a comfortable, upright position. Are you seated?

Great. Now, here is the Law of Attraction in the simplest way possible:

> *Whatever you think about the most, you will attract into your life.*

Sounds too simple? That's because it *is* that simple. Whatever you *focus on the most*—whether it's your dreams, worries or fears—you bring it closer to yourself.

Remember that famous dialogue from the movie *Om Shanti Om*, where Shah Rukh Khan says:

'Agar kisi cheez ko puri shiddat se chaho to puri kaynaat use tumse milane ki koshish mai lag jaati hai.'

This is exactly how the Law of Attraction works. But there is one thing that I want to bring attention to here.

You'll find the same idea in *The Alchemist* by Paulo Coelho. The book talks about a 'personal legend'—your biggest dream in life. When you truly believe in your dream and work for it, the Universe helps you in unexpected ways. This isn't luck—it's the Law of Attraction at work.

This is what the Law of Attraction is all about. And this is where our journey begins.

But wait—did you already take the first step?

Not yet! You missed the *Ready, Set, Go!* moment.

It's simple to learn about the Law of Attraction, but why do so many people struggle to use it? Why do so many fail to achieve what they truly want?

Here's the answer:

Knowing about the Law of Attraction and actually using it are two very different things.

Learning about the Law of Attraction is like packing your bag before a trip. It's just preparation.

But actually walking to your door, stepping outside and starting the journey—that's action. That's what makes the difference.

And that's exactly what we're going to do now. Now that you are starting to attract your dream life, why don't you tell me what it is that you are attracting?

Write five dreams that you want to manifest in the next 100 days; write as if this is your chance—this is the opportunity because God (the Universe) is watching and is ready to bless you:

1. ______________________________________

2. ______________________________________

3. ______________________________________

4. ______________________________________

5. ______________________________________

Day 2

The Secret Power of Gratitude

Hey there, good morning! We made it to Day 2! I hope you remember the instructions on how to read this book. One step at a time, one chapter a day.

Now, let me ask you something—do you remember Jay and Veeru from *Sholay*? Oh, of course, you do! Their iconic song 'Ye Dosti, Hum Nahi Todenge' is unforgettable.

Life is a journey, isn't it? And imagine how much easier and fun this journey would be if you had a Jay or a Veeru by your side. If you have one in your life, call them right now! Just say 'hello' and ask 'how are you doing?'; listen to the reply *and cut the call.* Seriously, do it! We'll laugh together once you're done.

But just like life, you also need a Jay/Veeru for your Law of Attraction journey. And here's the best part—you already have them. You just need to call on them.

How? you ask again.

Simple, I say again. Close your eyes and count to sixty. 1, 2, 3, 4 . . . Go on, count it down.

Done? Great! Now, think about something for a second.

- You were able to count from one to sixty—which means you know numbers.
- If you know numbers, you must know words as well.
- Oh wait, you're reading this book, which means you know English too!
- And because you're reading this book, that means . . . you're breathing.
- Which means you are alive!

Now, think about this question and answer honestly—when was the last time you actually felt alive?

When was the last time you looked at yourself in the mirror and said, '*Hey, that person in front of me looks awesome!*'?

The truth is, we often overlook what we already have. We get so caught up in chasing what's missing that we forget to appreciate what's present. But if you stop and think, there are so many things in your life that others dream of having.

And here's the magic:

'The more you are grateful for what you have, the more the Universe will give you.'

—Napoleon Hill

You see, the supreme powers—whether you call it God, the Universe or Energy—are always watching. And when they see you being thankful, they think:

If this person is already happy with what they have, imagine how much joy they'll feel when we give them even more!

But if you're always complaining, begging or feeling dissatisfied, they say:

No matter how much we give them, they'll still find something to complain about.

This is how gratitude works. The more you appreciate, the more abundance you attract.

So, let's sum it up in one powerful line:

The more you are grateful for what you have, the more abundance you will attract.

And today, your journey with gratitude begins. So, say *thank you* to five people today or tomorrow. DIL SE!

And, yes, I, Dr Amiett Kumar, your guide, mentor and friend, am grateful to have you all putting your trust in me and following this book with me to start your manifesting journey.

Day 3

Playing the Game of Manifestation: The MAGIC Formula

Congratulations!

You've crossed the first two days—clarity is forming, gratitude has begun—and now you're stepping into the field where the real *game* begins.

Do you remember playing **Snakes and Ladders** as a kid?

The rules were simple: ladders lifted you up, snakes pulled you down.

Manifestation works the same way.

Every time you practise consciously—meditate, visualize, affirm—you climb a ladder.

Every time you doubt yourself, delay action or compare your journey with someone else—you slide down a snake.

So how do we make sure we keep climbing?

By using the **MAGIC Formula**, the five invisible forces that turn thought into tangible results.

M: Mind Clarity

Think of your mind as a camera lens. When it's focused, everything becomes sharp and alive.

When it's blurry, even the most beautiful scene looks dull.

Clarity gives direction to energy.

If you don't know exactly what you want, how will the Universe deliver it?

Don't say, '*I want happiness.*'

Say, '*I am creating a life of emotional peace, meaningful work and loving relationships.*'

Write it. See it. Feel it.

Remember, your mind doesn't attract what you wish for—it attracts what you focus on.

When your inner picture is clear, your outer world begins to align automatically.

A: Aligned Emotions

The Universe doesn't respond to words—it responds to **vibration.**

And emotions are the purest form of vibration you emit.

If your words say, '*I'm confident*' but your energy says, '*I'm scared,*' the Universe reads the energy, not the sentence.

That's why emotional alignment matters.

Feel your desire as if it's already done.

Before the success arrives, embody the emotion it carries—peace, excitement, fulfilment.

Every master—athlete, artist, or entrepreneur—first *feels* the victory before they experience it.

Emotion = magnet.

The stronger the feeling, the faster the attraction.

G: Grounded Belief

Belief is the soil on which manifestation grows.

But even the best seeds won't sprout in shallow soil.

Grounded belief means faith rooted in reality— steady, calm, unshakable.

It's not blind optimism; it's inner knowing.

Affirmations like *'I'm abundant'* work only when your subconscious believes them.

So, nurture that belief daily.

Remind yourself of past proofs: times when things unexpectedly worked out, opportunities appeared, synchronicities unfolded.

These memories are evidence that the Universe has always been on your side.

When your belief stands firm, doubt loses its voice.

I: Inspired Action

Manifestation isn't magic without motion.

The Universe opens doors, but **you** must walk through them.

Inspired action means moving from intuition, not impulse; from inner guidance, not external pressure.

It could be a phone call, an email, a meditation, a new skill—whatever feels expansive.

When the action carries the frequency of excitement and trust, it magnetically multiplies results.

Don't wait for the perfect plan; start with the perfect *intention*.

Even one small, inspired step can shift an entire timeline.

C: Conscious Gratitude

Gratitude isn't just the finale of manifestation; it's the frequency that fuels the entire process.

When you thank life consciously, not mechanically, you anchor abundance into your vibration.

Each *thank you* sends a message to the Universe: '*I am ready for more.*'

Be grateful not only for what's visible but also for what's invisible: the lessons, the delays, the protection you didn't notice.

Conscious gratitude turns waiting into preparation and challenges into catalysts.

Say it out loud.

Write it.

Feel it, *DIL SE.*

Your Task for Today

Take a notebook and write **one line** for each letter of MAGIC that represents your current journey.

For example:

- **M:** My mind is clear about what I truly desire.
- **A:** My emotions are aligned with peace and possibility.

- **G**: My belief is grounded in trust.
- **I**: My actions flow from inspiration, not fear.
- **C**: My heart is filled with conscious gratitude.

Read them aloud. Feel them.

Each word is a ladder; each feeling a step upward.

Because once you live by **MAGIC**, life stops being a struggle and starts becoming a beautifully designed game you were born to win.

Day 4

The Blueprint to Your Dreams

Hi there! You're almost at the place where most people fumble or lose steam. You're moving past the turning point—just a little more, and you'll be doing what most people aren't willing to do.

Before we start, let's call our dear friend today. Sit comfortably, close your eyes and thank the supreme powers for everything you have. Take two minutes to do it right *now*.

Done? Good. Now, let's take the next step towards our dreams.

Whenever someone asks me, 'How do I use the Law of Attraction?' or 'Where do I begin?'—this is always the first task I suggest.

Are you ready to find out what it is? Hold on . . . Ready, set . . . It's *affirmations!*

Affirmations, journaling, scripting—call it whatever you want. It's a simple yet powerful way of putting your intentions out into the Universe.

Simply put:

An affirmation is a positive statement you write as if you have already achieved your goal.

But remember Day 1? Not everything that looks simple is easy. Affirmations are an incredible tool, but like everything else, they require effort.

I've met hundreds of successful people moving in the direction they desire. They all share one practice:

They write their affirmations.

But does writing something down really make it happen?

Let's put that to the test.

Go ahead—Google it or ask ChatGPT:

'What is the first step to constructing a building?'

Got your answer? I'm sure it's not about randomly showing up at the site and pouring concrete.

No. You need a design, a plan, a layout—*a blueprint.*

And affirmations work the same way.

Every time you write your affirmations, you're giving the Universe a clear blueprint of what makes you happy. That's when opportunities start coming your way—or better yet, you start creating those opportunities.

But wait! There's one thing that makes affirmations work.

And I bet, when you grabbed your pen just now, you missed it.

It's consistency.

This is what separates those who manifest their desires from those who don't. Writing your affirmations once won't do the magic. It's about doing it every day until it happens.

Remember the second rule of reading this book?

Miss one day, start again.

The same applies to affirmations.

Use any affirmation technique that suits you but remember, it only works when you do it consistently.

So, let's take action.

Write your first affirmation right now. But feel it as you write!

For example:

Thank you, God! I am driving my own Jeep Compass.
I am so happy!

Now, take a moment. Think about what you want next. Once you know, write your affirmation here:

____

And promise yourself today—you'll write this affirmation every day until it comes true.

Oh, and don't forget what we learnt on Day 3—take action!

You can write, 'I have bought my dream house!' every day, but it won't happen unless you take steps towards it.

So, what's your next move? Get writing. Get acting. Let's go!

Day 5

The Science Behind Visualization

Good morning! Time for a quick recap, don't you think? Let's go over what we've learnt so far:

- We now understand what the Law of Attraction is.
- We've made a great friend (gratitude) to keep us on track.
- We've learnt how to implement the Law of Attraction in real life.
- We've discovered how to communicate with the Universe and express our desires.

But wait—did we miss something?

We've told the Universe what we want, but are we clear about what we truly desire?

If you're unsure what I mean, don't worry—I've got you covered.

When you set a goal, you must bring it into existence by clearly defining it. Affirmations help communicate with the Universe, but visualization helps clarify things for ourselves.

> *The clearer your vision, the more focused your actions. The more focused your actions, the faster you manifest your goals.*

But is it really possible to achieve something just by thinking about it?

I had my doubts at first, too. But now, I can tell you with 100 per cent certainty—it works. And not only does it work, but it's also a method used by some of the most successful people in the world.

You might be surprised to learn that top athletes, actors and entrepreneurs swear by visualization.

Suresh Raina and M.S. Dhoni. Both legendary cricketers have spoken about picturing their match-winning moments before stepping onto the field.

Ryan Reynolds and Robert Downey Junior. Both legendary actors have credited visualization in interviews for shaping their best scenes and movies.

Steve Jobs (former CEO of Apple) and Elon Musk (CEO of SpaceX). Jobs was known for imagining Apple products long before they became a reality, while Musk was drifting through space since childhood; that was the thought behind SpaceX.

Gukesh Dommaraju. The youngest undisputed chess world champion has talked about his practice of visualizing his moves right before all his games.

In fact, a Harvard study found that people who visualized practising the piano for two weeks improved almost as much as those who physically practised it.[1] That's how powerful your mind-to-body connection is.

Let's say your dream is to own a house. How do you use *visualization* to attract it?

1. **Find visual references.** Look up pictures of interiors, designs or homes that match your dream house.
2. **Close your eyes.** Imagine yourself standing at your front gate.
3. **Walk inside in your mind.** Touch the walls, sit on the couch, feel the floor beneath your feet.

Now, think about this line:

I have my dream house.

When you think about this, the picture you just created will come to mind automatically.

Now, when you take action towards this goal—whether it's researching properties, improving finances or making a plan -your mind will be aligned with your vision.

Did you know? Your mind processes around *60,000 thoughts* every day. So how do you make sure this one thought stays in your subconscious?

- *Practise visualization daily.*
- *Be consistent—it's the fuel that keeps your journey going.*

Here is a quick tip for those who have reached this far:

The best time to visualize is **right after waking up** and **right before sleeping**. You will absolutely fall in love with this technique, and you will definitely start feeling closer to your dreams.

Are you ready to see your dreams before they come true? Then dream on.

Day 6

The Moment It All Began

So where were we last? Oh yes, we were at our dream house. Speaking of which, this reminds me of how my journey with the Law of Attraction first began.

It feels like yesterday when I stumbled upon a YouTube documentary called *The Secret*. I remember watching it, completely mesmerized. It was my first exposure to this world of possibilities. If you haven't seen it yet, I highly recommend checking it out—it's still available on YouTube.[2] I assure you, it will be a magical experience.

But here's the thing: Watching the documentary didn't mean I was applying the Law of Attraction yet. But something about it sparked a new kind of happiness in me, a feeling that I had never experienced before.

Then, when Rhonda Byrne (television writer and producer) released *The Secret* as a book, I read it cover to cover. That's when I started to truly dive deep into these principles.

The Secret helped me understand key concepts of manifestation—the power of thoughts, gratitude, belief and visualization.[3]

One of the most powerful ideas in the book is this:

'*Your thoughts become things.*'

This simple yet profound truth helped me understand how everything in our life is a reflection of our most dominant thoughts.

Rhonda Byrne explains in *The Secret* that your mind is like a transmission tower—whatever signals you send out, the Universe reflects back to you in the form of experiences.

The book also shares many real-life stories of people who used the Law of Attraction to manifest their dreams, from building businesses to attracting love and financial abundance.

After reading *The Secret*, I realized—this wasn't just a theory. It was real. And I wanted to experience it for myself.

When I finally started implementing the Law of Attraction, I learnt something crucial—positivity is not just a mindset; it's a tool.

I began practising gratitude, visualization and affirmations, just like the book suggested. And guess what?

I manifested my dream job at Bacardi as IT Head.

Now, I know what you're thinking—*getting a job is hard!* But here's something I learnt:

Manifesting a job is actually one of the easiest things to achieve with the Law of Attraction.

Why? Because jobs already exist. You're not trying to create something entirely new—you're just attracting the right opportunity towards you.

I followed the same techniques from *The Secret*, and the results spoke for themselves.

Even today, I always recommend *The Secret* by Rhonda Byrne to beginners. It's a great starting point for anyone who wants to explore the Law of Attraction and take their first step towards transforming their life.

And trust me, once you start applying these principles, you'll never see life the same way again.

Day 7

Celebrating Our First Week and Embracing the Power of Books

Today is going to be a great day. Wondering why? *Today is DAY 7!* Congratulations, everyone—we made it through an entire week!

Let's round it off, shall we? I want you to get back to the exact same spot you sit when I ask you to relax. In a comfortable posture with your back straight.

Great, now that you're relaxed and sitting upright, I want you to do one simple exercise:

Thank the Universe/God/supreme power you believe in. Call upon them and thank them for everything that has happened to you in the past week.

Take your time. Spend five minutes with your eyes closed and note even the smallest details that brought you joy, no matter how minor they seemed. Maybe you enjoyed a delicious meal, arrived at work on time or had a restful sleep. Even the tiniest moments that made you smile—express gratitude for them.

Go ahead, and when you're done, we'll move on to have some more fun today.

Today, I'm going to share something that has been a big secret to my success and the success of many others.

This one thing has propelled individuals to their pinnacle, helping them transform into the best versions of themselves.

Before I share this *brahmastra* with you, make sure you're ready to handle the ultimate power it holds.

Ready? Here it is—the ultimate tool that will help you reach your highest potential:

BOOKS

From ancient times, when our ancestors wrote on leaves and wooden planks, the written word has been one of the primary modes of knowledge transmission for us.

I have read over 800 books to date, and more than eighty of them were on the Law of Attraction, manifestation, quantum science and energy healing. Today, I'm going to introduce you to five of the most powerful books on the Law of Attraction. These are the books that have helped me achieve my goals, and I offer them to you to do the same:

1. *Ask and It Is Given* by Esther Hicks and Jerry Hicks
    This book delves into the concept that our desires are natural and meant to be fulfilled. Through the

teachings of Abraham, it explains how to manifest your desires by aligning with the natural laws of the Universe.

2. *The Science of Getting Rich* by Wallace D. Wattles

   Published in 1910, this classic explores the idea that believing in your desires and focusing on them can lead to their realization. Wattles emphasizes that positive thinking and faith are crucial in attracting wealth and success.

3. *The Power of Your Subconscious Mind* by Dr Joseph Murphy

   Dr Murphy discusses how our subconscious mind influences our actions and outcomes. He provides techniques to harness its power, suggesting that by changing our thought patterns, we can change our lives.

4. *The Secret* by Rhonda Byrne

   This widely acclaimed book introduces the concept that thoughts can shape reality. Byrne compiles insights from various teachers to explain how positive thinking and the Law of Attraction can bring about desired outcomes.

5. *Creative Visualization* by Shakti Gawain

   Gawain's work focuses on using mental imagery and affirmations to produce positive changes. She provides practical exercises to help readers visualize their goals and manifest them into reality.

These are must-read books to deepen your understanding of the Law of Attraction and assist you in reaching your goals.

Remember, the journey of a thousand miles begins with a single step. Embracing the wisdom within these books could be that pivotal step towards manifesting your dreams.

Happy reading!

Day 8

The Power of Words

Congratulations! You've worked hard for the past seven days, and today, we're going to learn one of the most important lessons in this journey.

I hope you have fixed a special spot as I suggested in the beginning; go and sit comfortably on that spot. Now, read each word with intent.

There is a famous saying among our elders:

सोच समझ के बोलना चांहिए, क्योंकि दिन में एक बार, सरस्वती आपकी ज़बान पर जरूर बैठती है।

Choose your words wisely, for once a day, divine energy flows through your speech.

Put it this way:

Once every day, the supreme powers listen to you. In that divine moment, what you say is what they hear.

Imagine you just had an argument at work, and out of frustration, you say, 'I hate my boss!'

Now, what if at that very moment, the supreme powers decided to visit you?

What would they think?

This person is talking about hate. Is that what they want more of?

Even if you spend the rest of the day in a positive state, the Universe only heard that one emotion—hate.

This is the power of words. This is why our elders always tell us to think before we speak.

Your words shape your reality—not just what you say to others, but what you say to yourself.

Let's understand this in depth. Have you ever thought:

- *Why is my life so difficult?*
- *Why am I not able to earn money?*

If you've ever asked yourself these questions, you'll understand why words matter.

When you phrase your thoughts negatively, your mind aligns with that negativity. Instead of finding solutions, you focus on what's lacking.

But ask yourself—if you have the ability to think about difficulties, don't you also have the ability to think about solutions?

We often don't realize the weight our words carry, and that's what we need to learn today.

That was a bit heavy, wasn't it? But don't worry—you're in safe hands.

Oh, wait . . . hands? Want to see a magic trick?

Try this:

'Wow, I have Rs 2000 in my account. I wonder how I can fill it to the brim. What's my account limit again? Rs 2 crore? That means I'm only Rs 1,99,98,000 away from my goal! Let's see how fast I can reach it.'

Do you see what happened? I could have thought:

- *I only have Rs 2000. How can I do anything with this?*

But instead, I reframed it as:

- *I have Rs 2000. How can I start investing to get more?'*

A simple shift in tone and wording changed everything.

Complaining: '*I only have Rs 2000. How can I invest?*'
Wondering: '*I have Rs 2000. What's the best way to start investing?*'

This slight change in words can bridge the gap between doubt and possibility.

If you focus on negatives, you'll feel anxious, frustrated and drained.

But if you reframe your words, you'll feel hopeful, creative and full of ideas.

This is called **self-affirmation**, and today, we're going to use it to reshape your reality.

Starting today, change how you speak to yourself:

- Didn't get selected for a job? GOOD! *Someone out there is waiting to hire me—they need me more!*
- Facing a challenge? GOOD! *I'm learning how to climb this mountain—who knows what lies on the other side?*
- Something not going your way? GOOD! *This is an opportunity to grow.*

So, remember:

Think before you speak. You never know when Saraswati ji will bless your words.

Activity: Redefine your LIFE:

Write five problems you are facing:

1. ____

2. ____

3. ____

4. ____

5. ____

Now rephrase these problems into positive statements that encourage you to overcome them just like we did on the previous page.

1. _______________________________________

2. _______________________________________

3. _______________________________________

4. _______________________________________

5. _______________________________________

Day 9

The Power of Positivity

A new day brings new perspectives, and today, we're going to start with a quick exercise.

Stand up for a minute and do ten sit-ups. Now, stretch your arms and jump ten times.

Done? Great! You're now active both physically and mentally. Feels refreshing, right?

Now, let's take a trip down Bollywood memory lane—do you remember *No Entry*, the classic comedy?

In that movie, Anil Kapoor's character, Kishan, keeps repeating a particular dialogue whenever he faces a problem. You've probably heard this line from family or friends too:

'B+' or 'Be Positive'

He was referring to his blood group, but let's be honest—the first time you heard it, you probably thought he meant 'be positive' as in having a positive mindset!

And that's exactly what we're discussing today—the true power of positivity.

Nowadays, people casually say:

'Just think positively and keep going.'

But why should you be positive? How do you stay positive? No one explains that part.

Let's break it down with a relatable example:

What's easier?

- Doing ten sit-ups and ten jumping jacks?
- Or staying in bed all day?

Your answer is probably staying in bed—because it requires zero effort.

Now, hold on to that thought.

When you're facing a challenge, it's easier to feel overwhelmed, stressed or doubtful—just like it's easier to stay in bed.

But the more you stay in bed, the more you lose the opportunity to get stronger and healthier.

Similarly, the more you sink into negativity, the harder it becomes to find solutions and move forward.

But here's the thing—is it really that hard to do ten sit-ups? No! It's just a small effort.

Being positive works the same way. It's a simple shift in how you see and respond to situations.

Just like we discussed on Day 8—reframing your words and thoughts makes all the difference.

The more positive you are, the more positive your environment becomes, and that, in turn, attracts abundance.

This isn't just a motivational quote—it's a fact, backed by science.

A study by Barbara Fredrickson, a psychologist at the University of North Carolina, found that positive emotions 'broaden and build' our ability to think, create and solve problems.[4]

Harvard researchers found that optimistic people had lower risk of cardiovascular disease compared to those with a negative outlook.[5]

In neuroscience, the reticular activating system (RAS) filters information. The more you focus on positivity and opportunities, the more your brain actively looks for them in the real world.

This means that positivity literally rewires your brain for success.

Here's the best part—positivity isn't one-size-fits-all.

Think of it like tea. Some people like it strong, others with more sugar. Similarly, what makes one person feel positive might be different for someone else.

- For some, it's watching a favourite movie.
- For others, it's listening to uplifting music.
- Some might find peace in nature or a picnic.
- Others feel positive by spending time with loved ones.

Find your source of positivity and make it a habit. The more positive energy you cultivate, the more abundance will be drawn to you.

So, what are you waiting for?
Shift your thought process.
Focus on positivity.
Spread it to your surroundings, family and friends.
That's how you attract abundance. That's the sugar
in your tea.

Now, here is a task for you: find the meaning of this
verse from Bhagavad Gita

कर्मण्येवाधिकारस्ते मा फलेषु कदाचन |
मा कर्मफलहेतुर्भूर्मा ते सङ्गोऽस्त्वकर्मणि ||

Consider this your homework for today.

Day 10

The Art of Letting Go and Surrendering to the Universe

Hi there, did you complete the homework I gave you yesterday? If not, then you just stepped on a snake in our snakes and ladders game! But don't worry, we can climb back up. Sit back in your regular spot, focus, close your eyes and perform ten sets of box breathing before moving forward.

Here is how you do it:

1. Inhale slowly to a count of five.
2. Hold your breath for a count of five.
3. Exhale slowly and steadily to a count of five.
4. Hold your breath again for a count of five.
5. Repeat the process ten times.
6. You can add a simple affirmation 'I feel so calm' between each cycle.

For those of you who found the translation of the verse, did you truly understand it? If not, I urge you to go deeper and study its meaning.

For those still wondering, here is the translation of this verse from the Bhagavad Gita:

कर्मण्येवाधिकारस्ते मा फलेषु कदाचन |
मा कर्मफलहेतुर्भूर्मा ते सङ्गोऽस्त्वकर्मणि || 47 ||

'You have the right to perform your prescribed duty, but you are not entitled to the fruits of your actions.'
(Bhagavad Gita—Chapter 2, Verse 47)

I am sure you have noticed a pattern by now—the universal principles we discuss seem simple in theory but hold infinite depth when it comes to true understanding and implementation.

Today, we dedicate ourselves to this one verse from the Bhagavad Gita. This verse is the true spiritual essence of *letting go* or *surrendering to the Universe.*

But what does it mean to *let go?*

Before we discuss *how* to let go, we must first understand *what* it means to surrender to the Universe.

When we were learning about affirmations, we called them the blueprint that we send to the Universe, detailing what will make us happy. In response, the Universe provides opportunities, ideas and paths to make those desires a reality.

However, many of us make one critical mistake—we become overly attached to the process.

We visualize, we affirm and we follow every technique diligently. But at some point, we must let go. Manifestation is not about obsession; *it is about faith*.

To understand this better, let's take the example of Aarushi, a young artist trained in traditional Indian art who applied for an art fellowship in Varanasi.

Aarushi started practising affirmations and visualization months before the results. Her daily affirmation looked something like this:

'Thank you, Universe! I've been selected for the Varanasi Art Fellowship! I'm painting beside the Ganga, surrounded by divine energy!'

For months, she followed this practice with complete devotion.

Then, the selection window closed. Her artwork was submitted. Her part was done.

Now comes the real question:

What should Aarushi do now?

She could keep writing her affirmations every day, hoping for a yes. But—the decision is already out of her hands.

At this moment, Aarushi has one more option to **surrender**.

She has done her part:

- She created a clear vision.
- She practised her affirmations daily.
- She visualized her dream life in Varanasi.
- She submitted her work with full faith.

Now, it's time to let go and trust the Universe.

This is where most people struggle. Instead of surrendering, they begin to overthink, doubt and stress about what is no longer in their control.

The Law of Attraction is NOT about controlling every step of the process. It is about aligning yourself with your desires, taking action and then having faith in divine timing.

Once you have taken action, you must detach from the outcome. Obsessing over *when* or *how* something will happen blocks your manifestation.

Think of it this way:

- Imagine planting a seed in your garden. You water it daily, give it sunlight and ensure it has the right conditions to grow.
- Now, what if you dig it up every day to check if it has sprouted? Would that help it grow faster? No! In fact, it might destroy the process.

The same applies to manifestation. Once you have done your part, let the Universe do the rest.

If you struggle with letting go, follow these simple steps:

1. Trust that your desire is on its way:
- Remind yourself: *The Universe is working for me, even if I can't see it yet.*
- Know that *what you seek is already seeking you.*

2. Shift your focus to the present:
- Instead of obsessing over the future, enjoy the present moment.
- Stay grateful, positive and open to opportunities.

3. Detach from the timeline:
- Stop thinking, *When will it happen?*
- The Universe delivers at the perfect time, not your expected time.

4. Keep taking inspired actions:
- Letting go does not mean doing nothing!
- Keep improving, keep learning and keep moving forward.

5. Replace worry with faith:
- Every time you feel anxious about your manifestation, repeat:

I trust the process. I trust the Universe.

Letting go is not giving up; it is having faith.

Similarly, your job is to align yourself with your desires, work towards them and then release your attachment to the outcome.

So, from today, trust in the process, surrender to the Universe and let go of your worries. Your dreams are on their way—just be patient and keep moving forward.

Day 11

Grab Your Ticket to the ATM

Uff, it has been a long walk, hasn't it? Have you ever played sports? I am assuming you raised your hand.

Well, if you haven't, then I will give you a reason to do it. RAISE YOUR HAND, EVERYBODY!

Good, now all of us have our hands raised. Now, with that out of the way, let's focus on today.

With your hand raised, I want you to say this statement out loud:

I am going to double my money by the end of next month.

Great, that's what we are going to focus on today. There is only one debate that mankind has had ever since we started living as a society:

What is it that a person needs to survive?

Some say food; others say water. Then there are people who think about clothes and a place to live. *The answer is air*; debate me on that.

Well, in all the arguments about clothing brands, housing prices, loans and interest rates, there is one thing that drives us all towards what we desire—a truly peaceful life.

What is that? It is money. It is the one superpower that we all possess. But there is always a feeling within that:

Ye dil mange more, Babu bhaiya!

(This heart desires more, brother!)

Don't worry, I got more for you. Here are five book recommendations to manifest money from me that will help you get the best out of your life.

1. *Think and Grow Rich* by Napoleon Hill
   This classic explores the power of thoughts in attaining personal and financial success. Hill presents thirteen principles, including desire, faith and persistence, to help individuals achieve their goals. A notable quote from the book is,
   'Wishing will not bring riches. But desiring riches with a state of mind that becomes an obsession . . . will bring riches.'

2. *The Map to Abundance* by Boni Lonnsbury
   Lonnsbury offers a comprehensive guide to manifesting wealth and joy by aligning thoughts,

emotions and actions. She emphasizes the importance of conscious creation and provides practical steps to transform one's relationship with money. A key insight from the book is

'The power to create anything already exists within us. You are no exception.'

3. *The Science of Getting Rich* by Wallace D. Wattles
    Wattles presents a straightforward approach to accumulating wealth, focusing on the idea that thinking in a 'Certain Way' can lead to success. He discusses the importance of creative visualization and acting with purpose. A pivotal line from the book states,

    'There is a thinking stuff from which all things are made . . . A thought, in this substance, produces the thing that is imaged by the thought.'

4. *How to Attract Money* by Dr Joseph Murphy
    Dr Murphy delves into the power of the subconscious mind in attracting wealth. He provides techniques to harness mental imagery and affirmations to remove mental barriers and invite prosperity. A significant quote from the book is,
    'Your subconscious mind is like a bank, a sort of universal financial institution. It magnifies whatever you deposit or impress upon it.'

5. *Secrets of the Millionaire Mind* by T. Harv Eker
    Eker explores the mental attitudes and habits that differentiate the wealthy from others. He introduces

the concept of a *'financial blueprint'* and emphasizes the importance of resetting one's mindset to achieve financial success. A standout quote from the book is,

'Give me five minutes, and I can predict your financial future for the rest of your life.'

These books offer valuable insights and practical strategies to help you cultivate a mindset conducive to wealth and success. By internalizing their teachings, you're well on your way to doubling your money and achieving your financial aspirations.

Now why don't we clarify our vision once:

1. Write the ten most luxurious things you want in your life.
2. In front of each object, write three actions you need to take.

____

____

____

____

____

Day 12

The Power of Dreams

Okay everyone, pack your bags. It has been a long journey so far, hasn't it? Why don't we take a detour and grab something fresh to eat? Sounds savvy, eh?

Great, let's go to this 'my favourite restaurant' place. It has some really good dishes. I heard the chef there can cook food from *every corner* of the world.

Are you following me? Good, do you know why I recommended this place?

Well, it was this small incident that took place the last time. I went there with my friend last week, but you see, everyone had told me that this chef was so good that he could fulfil all my desires for food no matter what, so I wanted to check it out.

So there I was, with my dear friend, and guess what, the chef recognized me and personally came to take my order. I told him I would love some noodles with the most unique sauces he could use.

He gave me a quick nod and went into the kitchen. At that time, my friend was feeling good about some south

Indian dishes; he found this unique dosa variety that I had never heard of and pointed it out to me. It was ten minutes after I had placed my order, and by that time I was enjoying my complimentary salad.

But the dosa variety intrigued me as well. So I said I wanted to have that instead of the noodles, since I'd had noodles before but never that one type of dosa.

I changed my order to the dosa that my friend suggested. We started talking about our college life and how there was this girl he liked. The two of them had gone out to this restaurant that was cut off from the rest of the places in Delhi.

He said that there he found the best dahi and paratha combination ever. He wasn't sure even this chef could beat it.

So I thought, *why not try it?* The description he had given me of the taste was so good that I wanted to taste it too.

So there we were, changing our order once again to the dahi-paratha combo that my friend had described. 'Stuffed to the brim and marinated in the best curd ever.'

By the time we had described our order, our third complimentary serving of salad appeared. We dug in and found ourselves munching without a thought.

After what seemed like an eternity, we were wondering whether we were going to be served or if our order had been misplaced due to so many changes. But alas, the order showed up, and it was the most out-of-the-world thing I had ever seen.

It was a paratha dipped in a bowl of sambar, served alongside curd that was definitely not white! And beside it were chopsticks in place of spoons and forks.

'What is this?' I demanded; I was pretty angry at this point. But then the chef explained what it was.

'It is exactly what you asked for. You wanted noodles, but with the most unique sauces possible, so I got some unique sauces ready, but by the time I was about to plate the noodles, you asked to have a dosa instead of the noodles. So instead of the noodles, I made the sambar ready, thinking that was what you meant. But by the time I prepared the dosa, you asked for a paratha instead and said, 'it should be stuffed to the brim', so I thought that is what you meant, and I stuffed the paratha in the sambar to the brim as requested.'

At this explanation, I was blown away. But then something blew me apart even more.

'Why does the curd look like that?' my friend asked.

'Well, the noodles are cooked in sauces, but since the paratha was supposed to be stuffed to the brim, I cooked the curd instead, so that you can marinate the paratha with it.'

Well, why am I telling this story to you? Hehe, want a clue? The cook isn't a human.

Did you get it? No? Ah, almost. This story is an insight into what your dreams are capable of.

The chef in this story is the Universe. It holds immense power; it can grant you all the things you can dream of (any dish that I can think of).

But did you get where I went wrong in that story? If you guessed it, then write it here and mention the day on which we discussed this:

____

Well, if you haven't figured it out, my mistake in that scenario was clarity and decision-making.

Here are the two things I did wrong:

1. I was not clear when I expressed what I wanted to the chef (the Universe).
2. I could not stick with what dish I wanted (my dream).

Did you get it? It is so easy to lose track of things in your day-to-day life that you don't know when the smallest mistake can cause an issue for you.

If you are leaving for a trip and someone says, 'I am worried we might lose a bag, so be careful'. The chances of you losing the bag increase dramatically compared to the situation in which that statement was not said.

That is how easy it is to lose track. Here is what I need you to take away from today:

Be absolutely clear about what you dream of, and *STICK TO THAT DREAM!*

It is such an easy thing to miss until one day, we get the weirdest dish served to us by the Universe.

The Universe has immense power; it is in our hands as to how we use it.

Make sure you do the activity below.

Write three clear dreams that you want to achieve.

____

____

____

Now look closely and analyse—what are you missing in your statements?

- If it is the colour of the car, mention it and visualize.
- If it is a house, then what is the size of it? How many rooms, bathrooms, halls, kitchens? What kind of furniture? Which city/state?
- If it is a life partner, what do they do? What is their speciality, what would be some thing they can do for you?

Got my point? Now rewrite those statements below and compare . . .

____

____

____

Can you see the difference?

Day 13

Nikola Tesla's Unique Gift

It's been a while, so let's check in on our dear friend—gratitude—once again.

Get up RIGHT NOW and jump five times on the spot.

Now, return to our daily spot, relax and focus. I want you to think of these three people:

1. A person you love the most.
2. A person who has helped you in a tough situation.
3. A person you prefer not to meet.

Got them in your mind? Good. Now, take a moment to thank them for existing.

I know, you might be raising an eyebrow for the third person. Why would you be thankful for someone you don't like? But here's the truth—every interaction, no matter how small, shapes our lives in ways we often don't realize.

Now that we've sent our gratitude, let's move on to today's lesson. Oh wait, did I spoil it with the title of this chapter? No? Good. Let's begin.

Nikola Tesla—one of the greatest pioneers of science. The mastermind behind the Tesla Coil, and the reason we enjoy electricity in our homes today. His discovery of alternating current (AC) changed the world forever.

But wait, we're not here for a physics lesson, are we?

Tesla had a technique beyond science, a method that aligns perfectly with the Law of Attraction.

It is called:

The 3-6-9 technique.

This powerful method is one of the most effective ways of manifesting your desires.

But what is the 3-6-9 technique, you ask?

Now, just because Tesla used it doesn't mean we need complicated math to apply it. All you need is the most powerful tool the Universe has given us:

WORDS

The 3-6-9 is an affirmation-writing technique designed to channel your focus and energy towards one goal.

How to do it:

1. Clarify your target. Define exactly what you want to manifest.
2. Write an affirmation around it, ensuring:

- It is written as if it has already happened.
- It starts with *'Thank you, God/Universe/supreme power.'*
- It ends with gratitude.

3. Choose three time slots daily (e.g., 9 a.m., 2 p.m. and 7 p.m.; the time may vary a little).
4. Write the affirmation:

- 3 times in the first time slot.
- 6 times in the second time slot.
- 9 times in the third time slot.

5. Repeat for forty-five days NON-STOP. If you miss even one day, restart from Day 1.

The one thing you *must not* do:

DO NOT CHANGE THE AFFIRMATION.

Once you choose an affirmation, *stick to it*. No alterations; no switching. The Universe needs a clear signal to respond effectively.

Ever since I started teaching this technique, people have shared countless success stories with me. And every time, I'm amazed at how powerful it truly is.

But why does it work?

It's simple—MINDSET.

When you repeat an affirmation daily, three times a day, your entire focus shifts towards that goal. You create strong vibrations, and these vibrations signal the Universe to align everything in your favour.

> *'If you want to understand the Universe, think in terms of energy, frequency and vibration.'*
>
> —Nikola Tesla

This constant repetition keeps you in a high-energy, positive state—and that's when manifestations happen.

If you'd like a more detailed breakdown, I have a video on this technique. Go check it out—and make sure to read the comments. You'll find some truly inspiring and heart-warming success stories.

Now, it's time for you to put this technique into action.

Are you ready to send your message to the Universe?

Here is a date card that will help you track your progress for the 3-6-9 technique.

	I	II	III		I	II	III		I	II	III
Day 1				Day 16				Day 31			
Day 2				Day 17				Day 32			
Day 3				Day 18				Day 33			
Day 4				Day 19				Day 34			
Day 5				Day 20				Day 35			
Day 6				Day 21				Day 36			
Day 7				Day 22				Day 37			
Day 8				Day 23				Day 38			
Day 9				Day 24				Day 39			
Day 10				Day 25				Day 40			
Day 11				Day 26				Day 41			
Day 12				Day 27				Day 42			
Day 13				Day 28				Day 43			
Day 14				Day 29				Day 44			
Day 15				Day 30				Day 45			

Day 14

Be Your Own Director!

Today we are going to expand our brain sizes a little bit. Just in case you are wearing a cap, loosen it so that your head can fit into it once we learn our lesson for today.

Excited? Yeah, that's what I like. Now, let's do a quick read of our dreams from Day 12, shall we? Go on and read them three times before we go on ahead.

Done? Let's get started.

Remember back on Day 5 where we discussed visualization. We glossed over a very keen technique that makes this method extremely powerful.

Today, we are going to study that point that we used but did not discuss.

Let's establish a baseline first. We discussed how **visualization** is one of the most powerful methods to implement the Law of Attraction. But how? Because it helps you gain clarity in exactly what you want. This helps you be direct, accurate and effective in the actions you take, and that in turn increases the speed at which you achieve your goals.

Good so far? Read once more to thoroughly understand. Now, back on Day 5, we discussed an example to explain how visualization works. That is what we are focusing on today.

It is called the **movie-making method,** and it is the most powerful visualization technique you can use and master.

Remember when we visualized our own house? I am sure you still remember the minor details from that day from that house. What we did that day was the movie-making method in action.

Here is the technique in a simplified way:

1. Each day when you wake up or before you go to sleep, you *visualize* yourself as if you are watching a movie.
2. In this movie, you are the hero, and the movie is going on **exactly** as you want your life to go.
3. You are achieving the goal the same way you want in real life.
4. You are reacting the same way that you would when it actually happens.
5. The hero (you) is achieving everything that you want in real life.

But as we keep saying, simple things aren't always simple.

Let's practise. I want you to go back to our dedicated spot and relax first. Now:

1. Close your eyes and remember the dreams you just read from Day 12.

a. Let's say your three dreams are: getting a good job, starting a relationship with the person you want and living a healthy life with them

2. Now, imagine yourself as the director of this movie.

3. Visualize the first scene; here it is the scene when you get your offer letter in the email. Visualize how you would react at that moment.

4. Now, shift the scene to a few days later and picture yourself in your favourite restaurant. You are giving the news to the person you want to start a relationship with.

5. Imagine the person's reaction as the way you would *want* them to react. Now, you confess your feelings to them.

6. He/she agrees, and the scene shifts to a later time with the two of you standing hand-in-hand at the front door of your brand new house, planning your first dinner there together as a married couple.

7. The scene shifts, and you see yourself sitting beside your partner in your old age, recounting your memories from your youth and laughing.

Now, slowly open your eyes. How do you feel?

Did it bring a smile to your face? That's the power of visualization. Using this method two times a day, once after you wake up and once right before you sleep, can do wonders for you.

What are you waiting for? Go direct your own movies. You already have the dreams you want to achieve; isn't that the best script you can imagine?

Activity:

Write your first dream script and let your dreams fly!

____

____

____

____

____

____

____

____

____

____

____

Day 15

Like Attracts Like—the Law of Magnetic Attraction

If you've been following along and reading between the lines, you might have realized something by now—I am a huge fan of *The Secret* by Rhonda Byrne.

This book introduced me to one of the most fascinating concepts that changed the way I see the world:

Like attracts like.

Now, let's think back to magnets for a second. As kids, when we played with magnets, we saw that opposites attract—the North Pole of a magnet pulls towards the South Pole.

But wait! If that's true, then why does a compass needle always point north?

Hmm . . . homework time! Go figure that out and come back to me when you do!

For today, we aren't talking about physics, but about how this concept applies to our minds and reality.

The idea is simple—*what you focus on grows*. The thoughts, feelings and energy you put out are exactly what the Universe mirrors back to you.

Let's test it right now with a fun experiment:

1. **Pick something to attract**—choose an uncommon object or colour, like a red car or butterflies.
2. **Set your intention**—say:
   'I am attracting red cars into my life. Thank you, Universe, for showing me red cars today.'
3. **Visualize for sixty seconds**—imagine seeing it around you—on the streets, in advertisements, in conversations.
4. **Go about your day**—don't actively search, just observe.
5. **Notice what happens**—within twenty-four to forty-eight hours, you'll start seeing what you focused on everywhere.

Here's the deeper truth behind this experiment—the Universe takes everything literally.

It doesn't judge, it doesn't question and it doesn't decide what's good or bad for you. It simply delivers what you focus on.

Think about it—if you constantly say

- *I always struggle with money.*
- *My life is so difficult.*
- *I never get opportunities.*

What happens? You attract more struggle, difficulties and lack.

But what if you flip the script and say

- *Money flows easily into my life.*
- *I am attracting incredible opportunities.*
- *Everything works in my favour.*

Your reality shifts.

Your thoughts are like radio signals—if you tune into negative frequencies, you'll only hear negative music. But if you switch the station, the entire tune of your life changes.

Now that you've understood how Like Attracts Like, here's your challenge:

For the next twenty-four hours, ONLY speak, think and write positively about yourself and your life.

Every time a negative thought enters your mind, flip it immediately.

For example:

I'm so tired today → *I feel my energy coming back with every breath.*

Nothing ever works out for me → *Things are aligning perfectly for me.*

At the end of the day, write down what changed—how did you feel? What small or big positive shifts did you notice?

This is your proof amiat that you attract what you think about.

The question now is—what do you want to attract next?

Day 16

The Power of Belief in Manifestation

So, did you find out why the compass needle points north? Did you discover that the North Pole is actually the magnetic South Pole of the Earth?

See how our schools have been fooling us since childhood? If the North Pole is supposed to be in the north, then why is the Earth's magnetic South Pole there?

There's a long history behind this concept, but let's save that lesson for another day. For now, I just wanted to get you in the right mindset for what we're about to discuss today.

When we talk about our goals and targets in life, where do they begin?

They begin from our dreams.

But before we go deeper, let me take you back a few days to something we discussed earlier. Follow me closely, okay? Let's not get derailed.

Remember this?

Like attracts like.

When we dream, we attract the things we dream about.

Are you with me here? Good!

Now, think back to when we visualized our dream.

Didn't you see yourself achieving your goal? Didn't you feel the joy, excitement and satisfaction of having it in your hands?

At that moment, you weren't just imagining your success—you were attracting possibilities, opportunities and people that could help you achieve it.

And without even realizing it, you also set yourself up to take action towards your dream.

Still following? Read again if at any point you miss the meaning.

Now ask yourself:

At any point, did you doubt yourself?

Did you ever think:

- *What if I fail?*
- *What if I mess it up?*
- *What if this isn't possible for me?*

If not, congratulations! You've already passed today's test. You've mastered today's lesson without even knowing it.

But if you did have doubt, then that's what we need to fix today.

Let's break it down with a simple analogy.

Imagine you're cooking a dish you've never made before. You have a recipe, the right ingredients and a clear vision of the final meal.

But the moment you start cooking, doubt creeps in.

- *What if I get the measurements wrong?*
- *What if this turns out horrible?*
- *What if I waste all my ingredients and have to throw them away?*

Because of this doubt, you start second-guessing yourself. You don't trust the recipe, you hesitate while following the steps, and in the end, your dish doesn't turn out great.

Now, imagine you believed in yourself completely.

You follow the recipe with confidence, enjoy the process and trust that it will turn out well. And guess what? It does.

The Law of Attraction works exactly the same way.

When you dream of something, you must believe that it is possible for you.

Doubt is like a brick wall that blocks your manifestations from coming through. Even if you do everything else right, doubt can cancel out all the energy you've sent to the Universe.

So, what's today's key takeaway?

Believe in your dreams as if they are already yours, and they will move towards you faster than you ever imagined.

Today, I want you to write down one dream you've been hesitant about.

Then, cross out all doubts and replace them with a statement of absolute belief. For example:

🚫 *I don't think I'll ever be financially free.*
☑ *I am attracting massive financial abundance every day.*
🚫 *What if I never find my dream job?*
☑ *My perfect job is already on its way to me.*
🚫 *What if my business fails?*
☑ *My business is thriving and growing effortlessly.*

Keep this statement with you today. Read it every time doubt tries to sneak in.

Because from today, we're not just dreamers anymore. We're believers. And believers always manifest their reality. We all start with low confidence; you will never cook the best meal on your first try. If you do, then you are a gifted cook. But if you don't, you simply keep trying until you get the recipe down to your memory.

When you are done, here is some homework for you:

Figure out what *aachman* (आचमन) means.

A hint for you: every pooja, or havan, uses this one concept.

Day 17

The Power of Water and Manifestation

So, did you figure out what aachman (आचमन) is?
Well, if your answer is:

The water that we drink three times during pooja and other traditional rituals.

Then you are close. But what does it actually represent?
Confused? Here, I will help you.
When I asked you about what aachman stands for, I wanted you to investigate why aachman is done. What is the thought process behind it, or what is the science behind it.
Have you ever wondered why we do this? Why did our ancestors and predecessors do this ritual? What is the logic behind this?

Here is the thought process behind aachman:

Aachman is a sacred Vedic ritual in Hinduism, symbolizing internal and external purification before prayers or rituals.

But how does this happen? How does this water have the power to help you align with the Universe and spiritually cleanse.

You already know the answer to this. How?

Next time when you sit in a pooja, just close your eyes for sixty seconds and focus on the atmosphere.

Did you feel that vibe? All the chants, all the rituals you perform, the offerings you make, the hymns you sing. It all emanates an amount of positive energy that is unparalleled to anything else.

When this water sits there beside you, all the energy that you emanate, the energy that these chants and rituals carry, is absorbed in this water and the water itself becomes a positive source of energy. That is where aachman comes into play.

See how beautiful the science from our ancestors is.

This phenomenon is also explained by a scientist known as Dr Masaru Emoto.

Dr Masaru Emoto's water research suggests that human thoughts, words and emotions *influence water's molecular structure*.[6] Through experiments, he found that water exposed to positive words, prayers or harmonious music formed beautiful, symmetrical crystals when frozen, while negative words led to distorted, chaotic formations. His work implies that consciousness and intention can impact physical reality, emphasizing the power of positivity.

But why am I telling you this? It is all to explain to you the thought process behind one of the most powerful manifestation techniques out there when it comes to aligning your energies.

It is called the **water technique**. It is actually the easiest technique that you can do for the Law of Attraction.

All you have to do is to:

1. Take a glass of water.
2. Hold it in your hands.
3. Think about affirmations that you want to be fulfilled. A good example can be: 'I have a healthy and fit body.'
4. Chant the affirmation with a positive mindset either by speaking, or by chanting it within your mind.
5. Drink the water.

Simple, right?

But do you know this simple technique has such magical effects that people to this day use this powerful technique.

Doing this as many times as you can, will *visibly* help you change your mindset and attitude.

So that is your task for today. Try this technique and just watch your mindset shift positively.

NOTE: You are supposed to think positively when you are performing this technique and do this as many times as possible.

Day 18

5x55 Magic

We've been working tirelessly day in and day out, so let's take today to simply calm ourselves and spend a few moments with ourselves.

Let's head back to the place we always sit around. Sit in a comfortable posture. Now I want you to follow this exercise for five cycles. It is known as the triangle breathing technique:

1. Take a deep breath in.
2. Hold for seven counts: 1 . . . 2 . . . 3 . . . 4 . . . 5 . . . 6 . . . 7 . . .
3. Release slowly in seven counts.
4. Now breathe in for seven counts.
5. Repeat from Step 2.

Here is a thought: When we were working with the 3-6-9 technique, it was supposed to take forty-five days, right? But my exam is in thirty days; what do I do right now?

Well,

'Where there is a will, there is a way!'

—George Herbert

And there is a way for you to manifest whatever you want in just **five days**.

I would like you to sit back in your comfy place and grab a pen and paper to understand this technique.

This technique is used when you are manifesting specific things that are time-bound or are way too near to use any other technique.

Here is how you do it:

1. Take a paper and pen.
2. Write an affirmation for the goal you are trying to achieve.
3. Write that affirmation fifty-five times.
4. This is to be done for five continuous days, right in the morning.
5. Take the actions that are associated with this task.

Simple as it comes. But note that this technique is very specific, so make sure that you write your affirmations with proper clarity.

Now, when does this apply?

Well, there are multiple use cases for this specific technique:

1. It can be an exam that is right around the corner.
2. An interview you are preparing for.

3. When you are planning to ask your crush out for a
    date.
4. You have a meeting to close a big deal in five days.

Basically, the goals that you want to achieve but are too
near to use any of the longer techniques. Pair this with the
movie-making method to clear your mind and improve
your focus towards your task.

This technique works on the principles of repetition,
focus and vibrational alignment.

* Writing an affirmation fifty-five times deeply imprints
  it in your subconscious mind.
* The number five represents change and transformation
  in numerology.
* The repeated action aligns your energy with the
  desired outcome and helps you take inspired action.

Try the 5x55 method!

Pick one goal that you need to achieve quickly. Write
your affirmation fifty-five times today and continue this
for five days.

Then, watch how the Universe aligns things in your
favour.

The faster you align your energy, the faster your
desires manifest! You can use this technique for anything
that is coming earlier or is nearby.

Day 19

Unlocking the Perfect
Moment to Manifest

Have you ever run a race? In the beginning, your energy is at its peak, your speed unmatched—but as the race progresses, maintaining that same momentum becomes harder. Life works the same way.

As the popular saying goes:

There is a right time for everything.

But if that's true, then when is the right time to manifest?

This question leads us to one of the most powerful techniques we've discovered on this journey. Have you figured it out yet? If you've been following along and practising with intention, you may have already started noticing subtle shifts in your days. A quiet transformation unfolding. Each morning, do you feel slightly different? More aligned? More aware?

But the real question is:

When is the ultimate moment to use the Law of Attraction?

We touched on this back when we discussed visualization—and today, we're diving deeper.

You might recall that the best time to visualize is right after waking up and right before you sleep.

But there's one moment more powerful than the rest.

Throughout the day, you face distractions—messages, calls, responsibilities, unexpected chaos. No matter how much you try to focus, life gets in the way.

But in the final five minutes *before sleep*, the world fades. The noise settles. Your mind enters a state of deep relaxation, free from interruptions.

This is your golden moment.

For just five minutes, claim this time for yourself. Out of twenty-four hours, this small fraction belongs **entirely to you**. No stress. No distractions. Just you and your vision.

And here's what you need to do:

Right before you drift into sleep, visualize your desires as if they are already real. See yourself living your dream life, achieving every goal, feeling the joy of success. Immerse yourself in that reality.

- Walk through your future like it's happening now.
- Feel the excitement of your manifestations unfolding.
- Declare to the Universe exactly what you want.

This is your time. *Don't let anyone take it from you.*

For the next eighty-one days, commit to this practice every night, and watch how your reality begins to shift. Your mindset will strengthen. Your manifestations will take shape. Your dreams will become tangible.

And when you reach Day 100, come back here and answer this:

How does it feel to live the life you once only imagined?

Your transformation has already begun. Keep going.

____

____

____

____

____

Day 20

The Power of Gratefulness

Hey there! I hope you're having a great morning today. Oh, and HIIIIII!

Didn't get it?

Go back and check 'Before You Begin'. Trust me, you'll feel extremely energized.

That's exactly how I want you to start this day—with joy and excitement!

Remember the friend we met on Day 2? The one who keeps you grounded, the one you should never leave behind?

Yes! We're talking about **gratitude**.

I hope you've been practising gratitude consistently, not just when we do it together but in your daily life as well.

But wait, if we already discussed why we should be grateful, then why are we talking about it again?

Because gratitude is not a one-time event; it's a way of life.

When you are thankful for what you have, when you keep talking to the Universe and expressing genuine appreciation, you become a positive magnet.

Remember what we talked about?

The Universe wants to give you even more when you appreciate what you already have.

So today, we call upon our trusted friend and *hamsafar* (companion) once again.

1. Sit down in your dedicated spot and relax.
2. Take a deep breath, hold for a few seconds and release. Repeat five times.
3. Look around and pick five objects. For example, a lamp, a pen, a pillow, this book, your watch, your phone . . . anything.
4. Hold each item in your hands and feel it.
5. Recall when you first got it and how you've used it since then.
6. Put each item back in its place, or someplace better.
7. Thank each of these objects for being in your life.
8. Sit back, close your eyes and reflect on how you feel.

Did that lighten your mood? Did you feel a shift in your energy?

That's how easy it is to change your vibe and elevate your internal energy.

This is the power of gratitude.

Imagine if you practised this every single day—your energy would be so positive that the Universe would naturally be drawn to you and work in your favour!

Gratitude is not just a self-help concept—it has been deeply embedded in Vedic wisdom for thousands of years.

1. Rig Veda (10.25.1)

यो नो मित्रस्य चक्षसा समग्रिर्देवो, अवृणीत प्रेष्ठः ।
स नः शर्म यच्छतु परावतः स यन्ता विश्वस्य धायसे नः ॥

One who acknowledges and expresses gratitude for the blessings in life attracts divine prosperity and abundance.

2. Bhagavad Gita (17.20)

दातव्यमिति यद्दानं दीयतेऽनुपकारिणे ।
देशे काले च पात्रे च तद्दानं सात्त्विकं स्मृतम् ॥

True gratitude is a selfless offering—one who gives thanks without expecting returns is always blessed by the Universe.

3. Atharva Veda (6.120.3)

यो नः सन्तोषेण तुष्यति स एव धन्यः;
यो नित्यमसन्तुष्टः स सर्वं लभमानोऽपि निर्धनः ॥

He who rejoices in what he has shall receive manifold; he who complains, even what he has shall be taken away.

Even in ancient Vedic rituals, offerings of gratitude were made before seeking blessings, proving that appreciation attracts divine grace.

When we practise gratitude daily, we are aligning ourselves with timeless, universal wisdom.

Rhonda Byrne, in her book, *The Magic*, takes gratitude to the next level.

She provides a twenty-eight-day gratitude challenge that rewires your mindset and shifts your vibration completely.

If you follow it, you will start noticing a transformation—from your thoughts to your reality.

From now on, I want you to call upon gratitude at every possible moment.

Gratitude keeps you grounded. It makes the Universe smile upon you.

And when the Universe smiles, it looks at you and asks: Is that what you want?

Tathastu!

Day 21

The Power of Vision Boards

Hey there! We're now a fifth of the way towards manifesting your dreams—congratulations!

For good record-keeping, let's note what we have been following for the past few days. Tick with a pencil the tasks you've been diligently practising:

* Daily affirmations
* Visualization
* Gratitude
* Book reading

Once you've checked the items off this list, sit back, take a deep breath and relax. If you've missed any of these practices, don't worry—you can restart them today!

Until now, we've been learning daily techniques that require consistent practice.

Today, we're switching gears—we're focusing on the bigger picture.

And speaking of visions—that's exactly what today's technique is about. This is a technique I personally use every year, and it's incredibly powerful for setting and achieving long-term goals:

The Vision Board!

A vision board helps you:

- Clarify your future goals and long-term aspirations.
- Set a visual roadmap of where you want to be.
- Train your subconscious to align with your desires daily.

Typically, vision boards are created at the start of each year. You place goals on it that you want to achieve by the end of the year.

For example, if you create a vision board on 1 January, your targets will be set for 31 December of that year.

This is where the long-term nature of this technique comes into play—it's about sustained focus and clarity.

Jack Canfield, co-creator of *Chicken Soup for the Soul*, credits vision boards as a key factor in his success. He used them to manifest a $100,000 cheque in his early days.

A study[7] found that individuals who vividly describe their goals in written form are significantly more likely to achieve them compared to those who only think about them.

These examples prove that when you see your goals daily, your brain subconsciously works towards achieving them.

Want to make one live with me? Join me on my YouTube channel; simply search for 'Vision Board by Dr Amiett Kumar' and I will walk you through a live vision board session. But for now, here's a step-by-step guide:

Step 1: Get your base.

- Take a sheet of yellow chart paper (the colour of positivity and abundance).
- Grab a red or green pen (sign of prosperity).

Step 2: List your goals.

- Write specific goals for the year, such as:

  o Buy a car; specify the model.
  o Move into a new house
  o Achieve a career promotion/dream job
  o Increase wealth and financial stability
  o Live a healthy life
  o Attract a relationship
  o Conceive a baby

Step 3: Find relevant images.

- If you want to lose weight, find the person who motivates you the most and paste their best picture there.
- If marriage is your goal, include an image of a wedding ring, a couple exchanging vows or a symbolic 'happily ever after' quote.

- If you want a car, print or cut out a picture of the exact model you desire.
- If you want a house, add images of interior designs, locations or floor plans you love.
- If your goal is financial success, add money-related visuals like cheques, bank statements or wealth symbols.

Step 4: Pin it somewhere visible.

- Your vision board should be placed where you'll see it every day—perhaps in front of your bed, study table, or office space, *where you see it all the time.*
- **Bonus tip:** You can write notes or affirmations beside your goals using a red or green pen for extra reinforcement.

A vision board is not just a collage of pictures—it's a mental reprogramming tool. It helps:

- Clarify your goals—so you don't get distracted.
- Train your brain to focus on opportunities that align with your goals.
- Remind you to take consistent action towards your dreams.

In simple words:

You manifest what you focus on.

This is why successful people swear by vision boards—because visualization is the first step to making dreams a reality.

- Create your first vision board.
- Look at it daily.
- Take inspired action.

Your future begins today—what will your vision board say about it?

Day 22

Law of Attraction and Action

HIIII!

Let's start our day with some light movement to boost our energy. Today's exercise is so simple that even a child can do it.

All you have to do is step outside, take a walk around your area and return.

Too easy? Okay, if you have a staircase in your house, try going up and down 100 steps—that works too!

Done? Good!

What? You thought all exercises were supposed to be difficult? Well, walking is an exercise too, isn't it?

Once again, I've used a simple example to get you thinking! Want to know how?

When I said, 'Let's start our day with an exercise,' what was your first thought?

You probably imagined an intense workout—push-ups, pull-ups or lifting weights.

But in reality, exercise can be anything.

- Remember your Class 10 maths book? The part where you solved problems was called 'Exercises 1.1, 1.2', etc. That was a mental exercise.
- Ever tried recalling multiplication tables from one to twenty? That's also an exercise—this time for the brain.
- What about the pen exercise eye doctors suggest? That too is an exercise for your eyes.

So why do we always assume exercise means extreme physical effort?

Because our mind functions on the information we feed into it.

And guess what?

The same applies to the Law of Attraction!

When I say:

You can achieve all your goals just by thinking about them.

Many people would immediately dismiss this idea—they would close the book and move on.

But not you.

You kept reading. You stayed curious. And that's why you're here.

Now, here's a big mistake most people make when trying to use the Law of Attraction.

They assume it works like magic—that simply thinking about their dream job, perfect partner or a million dollars will make it appear instantly.

But that's like watching Mukesh Ambani (Indian billionaire) step out of his luxury car and saying to yourself,

His life must be so easy.

Did you ever stop to count the hours, the effort and the challenges he overcame before stepping into that car?

Here's what happens:

- ⊘ People learn about the Law of Attraction.
- ⊘ They visualize their goals.
- ⊘ They wait for results . . . and when nothing happens, they say it's all a lie.

But here's the real question:

Did they take action before assuming the Law of Attraction had failed?

Because manifestation doesn't work without effort.

The biggest mistake people make is forgetting that action is part of the process.

Remember Day 4, when we discussed the five-step process of the Law of Attraction?

The most crucial step people miss is:

Taking Action!

Think of your life like a road trip.

- Your goal is your destination.
- Taking action is like driving the car to reach it.
- The Law of Attraction is your GPS—it shows the way.

Now, can a GPS take you to your destination if you don't start driving?

No!

You need to turn the ignition, step on the accelerator and move forward.

Today, I want you to truly understand what the Law of Attraction means.

Yes, it helps you align your energy with your dreams.

Yes, it guides you towards opportunities.

But in the end—YOU must take the wheel.

So today, take the initiative and start moving towards your dreams!

Day 23

The Magic of the Mirror Technique

HIIIIII!

Come on, say it back! I'll wait . . .

Good! Now that we've started with some energy, let's begin today's journey with a little experiment.

I want you to walk up to a mirror right now. It can be your bathroom mirror, a dressing table mirror or even your phone's front camera.

Done?

Now, look straight into your own eyes.

Not at your face, not at your hair, not at any imperfections you think you have—just your eyes.

Hold that gaze for thirty seconds.

Feeling a little awkward? A little strange? That's okay.

Because today, we're about to unlock a powerful Law of Attraction technique that has been used by world-class athletes, top actors and business moguls—yet so few people truly practise it.

The **mirror technique** is one of the most powerful manifestation tools out there. It involves talking to yourself in the mirror to:

- Reprogramme your subconscious mind
- Increase confidence and self-belief
- Align your emotions with your desires
- Raise your vibrational energy

Think of it this way—every single day, you talk to others. You give them advice, encouragement and appreciation. But how often do you talk to yourself with that same kindness?

That's why this technique works—it forces you to communicate directly with yourself.

The mirror technique is backed by psychology and neuroscience.

- **The self-perception theory:** (Bem, 1972)[8] suggests that we form beliefs about ourselves based on how we behave. When you speak positively to yourself in a mirror, your brain starts accepting it as truth.
- **Cognitive behaviour therapy (CBT)** techniques often use mirror exercises to help people build self-acceptance and confidence.
- A study by the University of Michigan found that people who used self-affirmation techniques in front of a mirror showed lower stress levels and higher motivation than those who didn't.

This means that speaking to yourself in the mirror isn't just 'feel-good' advice—it actually rewires your brain!

I want you to try this today. No excuses.

1. Stand in front of a mirror. Make sure you can see yourself clearly.
2. Look into your eyes. Don't look at your face, don't get distracted—just your eyes.
3. Start speaking positive affirmations. Here are a few examples:

    a. *I am powerful. I am strong. I attract success effortlessly.*
    b. *Everything I desire is flowing towards me.*
    c. *I believe in myself. The Universe believes in me.*
       Or, you are free to write your own affirmations.

4. Say each affirmation with emotion. Don't just say the words—feel them. Believe that you are talking to the most important person in the world—yourself.
5. Do this for three to five minutes every day. The more you do it, the more you will start to see the shift.

As mentioned earlier, Muhammad Ali, one of the greatest boxers of all time, talked to himself in the mirror before every match. He would say, *I am the greatest!*—and the world saw him become just that.

Lisa Nichols, before becoming a renowned motivational speaker, used the mirror technique daily. During tough times, she stood before the mirror and affirmed, 'Lisa, I am proud of you', 'Lisa, I forgive you' and 'Lisa, I commit to you.' This **mirror work** helped her rewire her mindset, build confidence and manifest success. Today, she is the bestselling author of books like *Amplify Your Life* and one of the most sought-after speakers in the world.

Serena Williams, the legendary tennis player, uses self-talk before every match. She stands in front of a mirror and affirms her belief in herself—and she dominates the game like no other.

These people didn't just wish for success—they spoke it into reality.

And now, so can you.

Today, I want you to do the mirror technique—for just three minutes.

- Look into your eyes.
- Say at least three affirmations out loud.
- Repeat daily for the next twenty-one days—and watch how you start feeling different.

Because here's the secret:

The way you speak to yourself becomes the way the world speaks to you.

So, tell yourself something powerful. Because the Universe is listening.

And when you look into the mirror tomorrow morning . . . what will you say?

Day 24

Clearing the Fog—Misconceptions

Another beautiful day to transform your mindset, isn't it? But before we move ahead, let me ask you something:

Have you ever heard someone say, 'The Law of Attraction doesn't work?' Or maybe, 'If the Law of Attraction was real, why aren't we all billionaires?'

If you've been practising everything we've discussed so far, you already know the truth—the Law of Attraction does work. But the problem isn't the law itself—it's the misunderstandings people have about it.

So today, let's clear the air and debunk some of the biggest myths about the Law of Attraction.

Misconception #1: All you have to do is think about it.

This is probably the biggest misunderstanding people have. They think just visualizing their goals is enough—that the Universe will magically drop success into their lap.

But let's get real. If simply thinking about wealth made people rich, wouldn't everyone be a millionaire by now?

- **Reality check:** The Law of Attraction is the GPS, not the driver. You must take action to reach your goal.
- **Example:** If you visualize getting fit but never exercise, will you suddenly have abs?
- If you want to be a great swimmer, can you do it without diving into the pool? No! The Law of Attraction works with your actions, not in place of them.

Misconception #2: Negative thoughts will instantly ruin everything.

How many times have you been told, 'Don't think negatively, or you'll attract bad things'?

Yes, positivity is important—but that doesn't mean one bad thought will destroy your manifestations.

- **Reality check:** The Law of Attraction isn't a punishment system. Occasional doubts or worries are normal. What matters is where your dominant energy lies.
- **Example:** Even the most successful people have bad days. What sets them apart is that they don't dwell on negativity—they redirect their focus towards solutions.

Misconception #3: The Law of Attraction is just wishful thinking.

Some people dismiss the Law of Attraction as pseudoscience or blind faith. But modern research actually supports many Law of Attraction principles.

- **Reality check:** Science shows that what we focus on expands; our brain is wired to look for patterns that match our beliefs.
- In short, the Law of Attraction works because your brain helps turn thoughts into reality through subconscious programming.

Misconception #4: The Law of Attraction means you can control everything.

A lot of people believe that once they master the Law of Attraction, they'll have full control over every aspect of their life. But that's not how it works.

- **Reality check:** The Universe works with divine timing and synchronicities, not instant demands. You can't control when or how something manifests—but you can align yourself to receive it.
- **Example:** You might manifest your dream job, but it may come through an unexpected opportunity rather than the path you originally envisioned.

Misconception #5: If it hasn't happened yet, it never will.

People often lose faith in the Law of Attraction when they don't see immediate results. They assume it isn't working simply because they haven't received what they asked for.

- **Reality check:** Some manifestations take time, and often, the Universe is aligning things behind the scenes. Impatience and doubt can block your progress.

- **Example:** Just because you planted a seed yesterday doesn't mean you'll see a tree today. Growth takes time, care and faith.

The Law of Attraction isn't magic; it's a tool to:

- Align your energy with your goals.
- Shift your subconscious beliefs.
- Open your mind to opportunities.
- Encourage action towards success.

When used correctly, it accelerates your journey, but you must be the one to take the steps. I have discussed some of these concepts in detail on my YouTube channel, 'Dr Amiett Kumar'. You can find in-depth explanations for this there as well.

Your dream life is waiting—are you ready to align with it?

Day 25

The Power of Self-Love in Manifestation

So today, we are starting with something that I suggest you do at least once a week.

I want you to disconnect from everything around you for the next five minutes.

Put your phone on silent, step away from distractions and find a quiet spot.

Now, place your hand over your heart and take a deep breath in . . . hold it . . . and slowly breathe out.

Now, ask yourself, 'When was the last time I truly appreciated myself?'

Because today, we are talking about one of the most overlooked yet powerful forces in manifestation—**Self-Love.**

The Law of Attraction works on alignment—your thoughts, feelings and beliefs must match the energy of what you want to attract.

But if you constantly doubt yourself, put yourself down or feel unworthy, what kind of energy are you putting into the Universe?

- Energy of lack.
- Energy of self-doubt.
- Energy of unworthiness.

And what happens when you vibrate at that frequency? You attract more of it.

Self-love isn't just about feeling good; it's about setting the foundation for what you believe you deserve. If you don't believe in yourself, how can you expect the Universe to?

Think about this—God, the Universe or supreme power created you.

If you constantly criticize yourself, doubt yourself or feel unworthy, aren't you rejecting that very creation?

The Bhagavad Gita (6.5) states:

उद्धरेदात्मनाऽत्मानं नात्मानमवसादयेत् |
आत्मैव ह्यात्मनो बन्धुरात्मैव रिपुरात्मनः ||

One must elevate, not degrade, oneself. The self is both a friend and an enemy.

Your relationship with yourself is the most important one you will ever have. When you embrace self-love, you align with divine energy, and when you reject it, you create resistance.

Would a painter appreciate you destroying their masterpiece? Would a gardener like you uprooting their plants? That's what self-hate does.

Self-love is not vanity or selfishness; it is respecting the divine creation that you are.

When you don't love yourself, you start a cycle of negativity without realizing it:

✖ Doubt → Fear → Inaction → Frustration → More Negativity

◐ You doubt your abilities → You fear failure → You hesitate to take action → You see no progress → You attract more failure.

But when you truly love yourself, the cycle reverses:

☑ Confidence → Belief → Action → Success → More Abundance

◐ You believe in yourself → You take action fearlessly → The Universe aligns opportunities → You attract success.

This is why every successful person practises self-love. It's not an ego boost—it's the key to unlocking their full potential.

I want you to try this simple exercise:

Take a moment to reflect—**Are you making yourself a priority?**

Prioritizing your health, goals and dreams isn't selfish. In fact, it's necessary. When you focus on nurturing yourself first, you can give more to the world. Your health and happiness are the foundation for everything you do.

Think of it like the airplane oxygen mask: you must put your mask on first before helping others. If you neglect your own needs, you'll have nothing left to give.

It's time to set boundaries, commit to your well-being and take steps towards your goals. You deserve this. Your time, health and dreams matter. Don't wait for the perfect moment—**start today**.

Day 26

The Divine Timing

Today, we start with a simple yet powerful exercise that will shift your perspective on life's challenges.

Now, sit in a relaxed posture, take a deep breath and write down *three things* that troubled you in the past week.

It could be a delayed opportunity, a failure, a tough conversation—anything that made you feel uneasy or frustrated.

Once you've written them down, put it in front of you and close your eyes. Take two deep breaths.

Now, I want you to rewrite each problem in a way that turns it into a lesson for your personal growth.

For example-

Problem: *I couldn't crack the deal with the client.*

Correction: *The Universe is preparing something even better for me, and I have the chance to upskill and prepare myself.*

Reframing problems this way aligns you with the Universe's wisdom rather than resisting it. Now, let's talk about something we all struggle with—the correct timing of the Universe.

If you've been practising the Law of Attraction, visualizing, affirming and taking action, but you're still waiting for results, I have something important to tell you:

Your desires are on their way. The delay does NOT mean denial.

But here's the catch:

Your frustration about 'why it hasn't happened yet' is actually pushing it further away.

When you say,

- *Why is it taking so long?*
- *I've been manifesting for months, but nothing is happening!*

You are vibrating at the frequency of lack and impatience. And the Universe responds by giving you more waiting, more frustration.

Imagine baking a cake. Would you keep opening the oven every two minutes to check if it's ready? No! You follow the recipe, set the right temperature and trust that with time, it will rise perfectly.

Your desires are the same: they need the right conditions, the right time and the right energy to blossom.

This is a question many people ask:

How long will it take for my affirmation or practice to work?

The answer? **Divine Timing.**

Everything in the Universe follows a natural rhythm. The sun rises at its perfect time, the seasons change when they are meant to, and a baby is born after exactly nine months of development.

Would you try to force a fruit into ripening before its time? No, because it would be bitter.

Similarly, forcing a manifestation before its time will not bring the right results.

You are not being denied what you want. You are being prepared to receive it in its highest and best form.

As mentioned earlier, the Bhagavad Gita beautifully explains the essence of patience and surrender in this shloka:

कर्मण्येवाधिकारस्ते मा फलेषु कदाचन ।
मा कर्मफलहेतुर्भूर्मा ते सङ्गोऽस्त्वकर्मणि ॥

You have a right to perform your duty but never to its fruits. Do not be attached to the results of your work, nor be attached to inaction.

Your job is to act, to believe, to keep going. The results? They will come when the Universe decides it is the right time.

Now, I won't give you the meaning of the next shloka I want you to read. That's your task today.

Here it is:

सर्वधर्मान्परित्यज्य मामेकं शरणं व्रज ।
अहं त्वां सर्वपापेभ्यो मोक्षयिष्यामि मा शुचः ॥

Abandon all varieties of duties and simply surrender unto Me alone. I shall deliver you from all sins. Do not fear.

Find the meaning of this verse. Reflect on how it applies to surrendering to divine timing.

If you are wondering, 'Why is my manifestation taking so long?', remind yourself:

- The Universe is aligning everything perfectly for you.
- The right thing at the wrong time is the wrong thing.
- You are not waiting; you are growing into the person who will receive your desire.

Stay patient. Stay faithful. What you seek is seeking you too—it's just waiting for the perfect moment.

Day 27

The 10×3 Affirmation Technique

Let's start today by centring ourselves with a simple meditation that will take just ten to fifteen minutes but will leave you feeling focused, calm and ready for today's lesson.

Guided meditation for clarity and focus:

1. **Find a quiet space:** Sit comfortably, either on a chair or on the floor. Keep your back straight and hands resting on your knees.
2. **Close your eyes and take deep breaths:** Inhale deeply through your nose, hold for a few seconds and slowly exhale through your mouth. Do this five times.
3. **Focus on your breath:** Let go of any distractions. Feel the air flowing in and out, calming your mind.
4. **Visualize a white light:** Imagine a soft white light surrounding you, filling you with peace, positivity and focus.
5. **Set your intention:** Silently say, *I am open to receiving clarity, guidance and success today.*

6. **Gently open your eyes:** Take a moment to feel present before moving ahead.

Now that your mind is clear, let's dive into one of the most effective affirmation techniques—the 10×3 affirmation method.

The 10×3 method is a structured way to programme your subconscious mind using repetition and focused intention.

- Pick three dreams that you want to achieve. Give yourself time, focus on the dreams, visualize and obtain proper clarity.
- These dreams can be related, or three completely different goals you want to achieve.
- Now write one affirmation for each of these three dreams.
- Now each morning, give yourself proper time; don't think of this as a task you have to do. Dedicate time to yourself for this daily in the morning after all your other spiritual practices and write these three affirmations (three for each dream) ten times each. So, three affirmations ten times each—thirty affirmations in total. Done with focus, pouring all your heart and soul.

This simple yet powerful routine helps reinforce your belief system and aligns your energy with your goals.

Affirmations are not just words—they are commands to your subconscious mind.

- Dr Bruce Lipton, a renowned cellular biologist, states that 95 per cent of our daily actions are controlled by the subconscious mind.[9] By repeating affirmations, we reprogramme the subconscious to believe and act according to the new reality we want to create.
- Neuroplasticity (the brain's ability to rewire itself) plays a key role. Repeated affirmations strengthen neural pathways, making positive beliefs and habits automatic over time.
- Psychologist Claude Steele's self-affirmation theory[10] suggests that affirmations help us reduce stress, increase confidence and reinforce a strong self-image.

In short, what you say repeatedly, your brain starts accepting as truth. Try doing this exercise to test this for yourself:

If you've ever memorized a song without even trying, it's because of repetition. The same principle applies to affirmations—when you repeat something enough times, it sticks.

Bruce Lee, the legendary martial artist and actor, strongly believed in the power of the mind. He once wrote,

'As you think, so shall you become.'

They didn't wait to believe in themselves after success—they spoke it into existence first.

- Your beliefs shift. Instead of doubting your potential, you start acting as if success is inevitable.

- Your mindset becomes solution-oriented. You naturally start seeing opportunities where you once saw obstacles.
- Your energy attracts aligned experiences. The Universe responds to certainty and clarity, and this method helps you build both.

The 10x3 affirmation technique is simple yet life-changing—all it takes is commitment.

Day 28

Meditative Visualization—Deepening the Practice

Before we dive into today's lesson, let me ask you a simple question:

Have you been practising your daily visualizations correctly?

If yes, that's fantastic! You are already on the path to mastering the Law of Attraction. But if not, today is the perfect day to start.

Let's begin with a ten-minute meditation to get into the right mindset for deeper visualization.

1. **Find a quiet space:** Sit comfortably, close your eyes and relax your shoulders.
2. **Take deep breaths:** Breathe in slowly, hold for a moment and exhale completely. Repeat this five times.
3. **Become aware of your body:** Notice how your feet touch the floor and how your chest rises and falls. Feel the tension leaving your body.

4. **Listen to the silence:** Instead of focusing on external sounds, listen to the rhythm of your own breath.
5. **Repeat a calming affirmation:** Silently say, *I am calm, focused and connected to the Universe.*
6. **Visualize a gentle wave:** Imagine a peaceful wave of golden light flowing from the top of your head to the tips of your toes, washing away distractions.
7. **Open your eyes slowly:** When you feel fully present, gently open your eyes and bring this sense of peace with you.

Now that we are in a relaxed and focused state, let's take visualization to the next level.

Visualization is something you have already been practising every day. But today, we go deeper and not just imagine but fully experience our desires in a meditative state.

- Meditation opens your subconscious mind, making visualization more powerful.
- The deeper the experience, the stronger the manifestation energy you create.
- Your mind and body begin responding as if your dream is already happening.

Einstein's Theory of Thought Experiments

Albert Einstein believed that imagination is the key to innovation. He would visualize complex physics problems in his mind before proving them mathematically.

Basketball Experiment by Dr Blaslotto

In a famous study,[11] three groups practised free throws:

- Group 1 physically practised every day.
- Group 2 only visualized practising.
- Group 3 did nothing.
  After thirty days, the group that only visualized improved almost as much as those who physically practised.

Hollywood star Will Smith openly credits visualization for his success, stating:

> *'In my mind, I've always been a Hollywood star. I had to see it before anyone else could.'*

These examples prove one thing—when you deeply visualize your goals, your mind treats them as real, and the Universe aligns to make them happen.

1. **Get into a calm state:** Repeat the meditation we did earlier or take deep breaths to relax.
2. **Imagine your future self:** Picture yourself one year from today. What do you look like? What are you doing? How does success feel?
3. **Add details to the scene.** If you want:

   a. **A thriving career**—imagine yourself sitting in your dream office, receiving an award or giving a speech.

b. **A perfect relationship**—see yourself sharing joyful moments, travelling or celebrating milestones.
c. **Peak health**—feel the strength in your body as you exercise, climb mountains or dance with energy.
d. **Engage all five senses**—what do you hear? What scents are around you? How does the environment feel? The richer the experience, the faster it manifests.
e. **Express gratitude**—whisper, '*Thank you, Universe, for making this my reality.*
f. **Stay in the feeling**—hold on to this emotion of joy, success and gratitude for a few minutes before slowly opening your eyes.

You train your subconscious to recognize success as your new reality. Your brain creates neural pathways that attract the right people and opportunities. You eliminate resistance by already *experiencing* your success before it arrives.

Tonight, before you sleep, try this deep visualization exercise. Do this consistently, and you'll notice faster results, stronger confidence and a clearer vision of your future.

Day 29

The Power of Emotions

Have you ever noticed how your mood can shape your entire day?

You wake up feeling happy, and everything seems to go your way. But on the days you feel irritated, things start going wrong one after another. It's almost as if the Universe is responding to the energy you're putting out.

Now, think about your manifestation process. If emotions can shape something as simple as your daily experiences, what happens when you remove emotions from your desires?

The truth is the Law of Attraction does not work without emotions. Worse, if you allow negative emotions to enter your manifestation process, you may attract the opposite of what you desire.

Let's break this down in terms of actions and reactions.

Every thought you project carries a specific energy frequency. The Universe does not understand words; it understands energy and emotion.

If you visualize your dream life but feel indifferent about it, the energy is weak. The Universe registers that you don't truly care, so it does not prioritize that manifestation.

If you desire wealth but secretly fear money, your energy is conflicting. The Universe sees your doubt and reinforces your existing financial struggles.

Action: You think about a goal but feel nothing.
Reaction: The Universe sees no strong signal to respond to.

Action: You desire something but worry it won't happen.
Reaction: The Universe matches your doubt and delays your manifestation.

When you first start practising the Law of Attraction, emotions naturally fuel your desires. The excitement of imagining a dream life, the thrill of new possibilities, the joy of attracting something wonderful—all of this creates high vibrational energy.

But what happens when that excitement fades?

- You start feeling like manifestation isn't working.
- You repeat affirmations without any emotional connection.
- Your visualization becomes a mechanical habit rather than an immersive experience.

This is where manifestation weakens. Without emotions, your desires become empty signals that the Universe doesn't recognize as urgent or important.

Think of it like sending a message without pressing 'send'. The thought exists, but it never reaches its destination.

Now let's discuss something even more critical—what happens when negative emotions enter your manifestation process?

Let's say you've been visualizing success, but deep inside, you start feeling:

- Frustration that it's taking too long.
- Doubt about whether you deserve it.
- Fear that something will go wrong.

What do you think happens?

The Universe picks up on your dominant energy, not your words. So even if your thoughts are saying, *I am manifesting my dream life,* your emotions might be saying,

But what if it never happens?

And guess what? The Universe listens to the stronger signal—the emotion, not the thought.

The famous psychologist Carl Jung once said:

'What you resist, persists.'

If your manifestation process is filled with worry, fear and resistance, the Universe keeps sending you more reasons to feel those emotions.

So, what should you do if you notice that your emotions are weakening or turning negative?

- **Reconnect with your 'why':** Remind yourself why you wanted this goal in the first place. The excitement you felt in the beginning? Bring it back!
- **Feel before you see:** Your emotions should not depend on whether your manifestation has happened yet. Feel the happiness NOW. The Universe responds to what you feel, not what you see.
- **Take inspired action:** Nothing fuels excitement more than progress. If your manifestation feels stagnant, do something that brings you closer to it.
- **Eliminate frustration:** If you feel impatient, shift your focus. Instead of thinking, *Why hasn't it happened?* say,

I trust that everything is unfolding perfectly for me.

- **Gratitude resets negative energy:** If doubt and frustration creep in, immediately list five things you're grateful for. Gratitude shifts you back to a positive frequency.

Identify one goal you have been visualizing or affirming.

Reflect: What emotions do you truly feel about it? Are they exciting and confident? Or doubtful and impatient? If there are negative emotions, apply the above techniques to realign.

Manifestation isn't just about thinking; it's about feeling. And when your emotions match your desires, the Universe has no choice but to deliver.

Keep the emotions alive and watch your reality shift.

Day 30

Manifesting Weight Loss with the Law of Attraction

Did you know that over 90 per cent of people give up on their weight loss journey within the first thirty days?

They start with motivation, but the moment they don't see instant results, they fall into frustration and self-doubt.

But the truth is—**weight loss isn't just about food and exercise. It's also about mindset.**

No, I'm not saying you can *wish the fat away*. But without mental alignment, even the best workout plan feels like punishment. With the Law of Attraction, you turn the journey into something that feels natural, joyful and even exciting.

Let me share a moment that changed everything for me.

During a live session, someone asked if the Law of Attraction helps with weight loss. I replied, 'Yes, it does.' And then someone casually asked, **'If it works, why don't you use it?'**

That one question struck a deep chord.

I realized I had tried many times to lose weight—but never *truly* committed with belief and alignment. That day, I made a decision:

This time, I will use the Law of Attraction the right way.

I set a goal to bring my weight down to 90 kg. Then I did what I teach:

- I wrote the affirmation: **'Thank you, God! I am currently at 90 kgs!'**
- I visualized myself feeling light, fit and energetic.
- I did the **Water Technique**—charging water with my affirmation and drinking it with intention.
- I used the **Mirror Technique**, saying it aloud while looking at myself.

What happened next was incredible. I started noticing new videos popping up—on intermittent fasting, on walking, on light routines, home-cooked food, etc. These things were *always* there, but now I saw them with new energy.

- I followed intermittent fasting.
- I ate only between 11 a.m. and 7 p.m.
- I only ate home food. No junk.
- I did light walking. That's it.

In just **two months**, I went from **100** to **90 kg**. No gym. No crash diets. Just belief, alignment and consistent action.

This is how the Law of Attraction supports you. Here's a simple three-step Law of Attraction workflow to manifest weight loss:

1. **Clarify the goal**
   Know exactly what you want. Be specific. I wasn't vague—I said, '90 kg.'

2. **Use the Law of Attraction techniques**
   Use affirmations daily. Visualize the version of you who already lives in that body. Charge your water. Talk to yourself with belief in the mirror.

3. **Take inspired action**
   You'll start noticing ideas, videos and advice show up in your life. Don't ignore them—act on them. I did. That's what made the difference.

The Law of Attraction isn't a shortcut. It's a **mindset** that keeps you **focused**, **committed** and **joyful** so the journey becomes natural and lasting.

Your transformation has already started.

Now align your energy—and let your body follow.

Day 31

Mindfulness vs Overthinking—the Silent Battle of the Mind

Let's begin with something fun—a brain teaser for you!

Read the sentence below and count how many times the letter 'F' appears:

'Finished files are the result of years of scientific study combined with the experience of many experts.'

Got your answer? Take a moment, and count carefully.

Now, let me ask—did you find three? Or maybe four?

Well, the actual number is six. Surprised? Most people miss the F's in 'of' because the brain processes them differently.

This is how our mind works—we think we are aware, but often, we overlook details, get lost in thought or misinterpret reality.

And this brings us to today's topic.

Overthinking vs Mindfulness

Overthinking happens when your mind is stuck in multiple places at once.

- You are physically present but mentally absent.
- You are eating but thinking about work deadlines.
- You are working but stressed about personal problems.
- You are spending time with family but distracted by emails.
- You are relaxing, but your mind is replaying a conversation from yesterday.

Does this sound familiar?

Overthinking is when your mind refuses to stay in the present. Instead, it either dwells on the past or worries about the future.

Over time, this leads to:

- **Stress and anxiety,** because your brain is constantly running.
- **Decision fatigue,** because you think so much that even small choices feel overwhelming.
- **Missed experiences,** because you are physically there but mentally somewhere else.

Now, let's shift gears and talk about mindfulness.

Mindfulness is the opposite of overthinking.

It is the practice of being fully present in the moment, aware of your actions, thoughts and surroundings without judgement.

- When eating, you focus on the taste, texture and aroma.
- When working, you concentrate only on the task at hand.
- When spending time with loved ones, you enjoy their company without distractions.
- When relaxing, you truly rest without guilt.

Mindfulness grounds you in the present moment, helping you experience life fully and with clarity.

It is a state of awareness where you:

- Observe thoughts without attachment.
- Respond, rather than react, to situations.
- Train your mind to focus on one thing at a time.

If overthinking scatters your energy, mindfulness aligns it.

The Law of Attraction requires a clear, focused mind because:

- Your manifestations depend on the energy you give. If your thoughts are scattered, your signals to the Universe are weak.
- If you constantly doubt, worry or get distracted, you delay your manifestations.
- Mindfulness strengthens belief. The more present you are, the easier it is to visualize, affirm and act on your desires.

So today, practise one simple mindfulness exercise:

1. When drinking water, pay attention to how it feels in your mouth and throat.
2. When walking, observe your steps and surroundings without distraction.
3. When talking to someone, listen fully instead of preparing your next response.

The more mindful you become, the stronger your manifestations will be.

Remember, the Universe doesn't respond to noise. It responds to clarity.

So, take a deep breath, let go of distractions, and start attracting with focus.

Day 32

Clarity—The Ultimate Key to Manifestation

Let's begin today with a simple gratitude exercise to ground ourselves before we dive into today's topic.

1. Take a deep breath in . . . hold for a moment . . . and slowly exhale. Repeat this three times.
2. Look around you and find five things you are grateful for. They can be simple—your cosy chair, the sunlight coming through your window, the warmth of your tea or even this book in your hands.
3. For each one, say aloud or in your mind: *Thank you for being part of my life. You make my life richer in ways I never noticed before.*
4. Now, reflect on one major challenge in your life. Instead of seeing it as a problem, ask yourself: *How has this situation helped me grow?*
5. End with this affirmation: *I am grateful for everything I have. I trust that everything is happening for my highest good.*

Do you feel a shift in your energy? That's the magic of gratitude! It aligns you with abundance and makes you receptive to what the Universe has in store for you.

Now, let's take this energy and dive deep into the most critical element of manifestation—**clarity**.

If there is one thing that separates successful manifestations from wishful thinking, it's absolute clarity.

The Law of Attraction doesn't work with vague desires. It works with precisely defined goals.

Imagine you walk into a restaurant and tell the waiter, 'Bring me something nice.' What do you think will happen?

- You may get something you don't like.
- You may get something completely unexpected.
- You may get nothing at all because the waiter is confused about what to bring.

Now, imagine you say, 'I want a paneer butter masala with garlic naan and a fresh lime soda.' The order is clear, the waiter knows exactly what to bring, and it will arrive faster.

This is exactly how the Universe works. The more specific your order, the better the Universe can deliver it.

If you are feeling stuck in your manifestations, ask yourself:

1. Do I truly know what I want?
- Many people say they want happiness, success, or wealth—but what does that mean for them?
- Happiness could mean freedom for one person, while for another, it could mean being surrounded by loved ones.

2. Am I sending mixed signals?
*   One day you want to be an entrepreneur; the next day you consider taking a full-time job.
*   One day you affirm *I am in a loving relationship*; the next day you say *Maybe I'm meant to be alone*.
*   If you keep changing your order, how can the Universe deliver?

3. Am I focused on what I want or what I don't want?
*   If you say *I don't want to be broke*, the Universe only hears *broke*.
*   Instead, say, *I am financially free and abundant*.

Write down your desires in detail

Instead of *I want a new car*, write:

I am driving a brand-new white Toyota Fortuner with black leather seats, feeling proud and excited as I take it for a ride on a beautiful road.

Instead of *I want to be rich*, write *I earn Rs 10 lakh per month doing work I love, living comfortably and investing wisely*.

*   Use the **why** technique. For every desire, ask yourself:
    o   *Why do I want this?*
    o   *How will I feel when I have it?*
    o   *What will this add to my life?*
        The more emotional connection you have, the stronger your manifestation energy.

- Use visualization with clarity.
  - Close your eyes and see your goal as if it's already real.
  - Where are you? What are you doing? Who is with you? What does it feel like?
  - The clearer the image, the more powerful the manifestation.

- Align your actions with your desires.
  - If you want a dream job, are you applying for positions?
  - If you want a healthy body, are you eating nutritious food and moving your body?
  - Manifestation requires action! The Universe opens doors, but you have to walk through them.

Every single day, remind yourself:

- I know exactly what I want.
- I trust the Universe is aligning everything for me.
- I take inspired action towards my desires.

When you combine clarity, belief and action, the Universe has no choice but to deliver.

Now, let's take one step closer to our dreams—

- In the lines provided below, write your top three desires in absolute detail.
  - ____

____

____

o   _______________________

____

____

o   _______________________

____

____

- Feel them as real.
- Say aloud, *I am ready for my desires to manifest.*

Your order is placed, your clarity is strong and your manifestation is in motion.

Day 33

The Power of a Written Dream

There was once a struggling young actor in Hollywood, a man with dreams far bigger than his reality. He had moved to the city of stars, filled with ambition but barely making ends meet.

Every night, he would drive up to Mulholland Drive, a scenic hilltop overlooking Los Angeles, park his beat-up car and stare at the dazzling city lights below. To many, they were just lights—ordinary street lamps illuminating the roads—but to him, they were the symbols of something greater.

He saw his future in those lights.

One night, in an act of pure belief, he did something unusual.

He took out a blank cheque, wrote down an amount that seemed almost impossible at the time—$10 million—and dated it exactly five years into the future.

Under the memo line, he wrote:

'For acting services rendered.'

Why?

Because he believed that if he kept seeing it, feeling it and focusing on it, the Universe would find a way to bring it into his life.

Every single day, he carried that cheque in his wallet. He visualized cashing it. He affirmed that the money was already his. He put absolute faith in the process, even though, at that time, he was barely surviving on small comedy gigs.

Years passed. He still wasn't a huge name in Hollywood, but he refused to lose faith.

He took whatever roles he could find, poured himself into his craft and kept visualizing his breakthrough moment. He did not allow doubt to creep in.

Then, one day, everything changed.

A movie deal landed in his lap—one that would pay him exactly $10 million.

The movie? *Dumb and Dumber*.

The struggling actor? Jim Carrey.

And the cheque?

He finally had enough money to replace it with the real thing.

Jim Carrey wasn't just wishing. He wasn't hoping for luck. He took action, kept his belief strong and aligned his thoughts with his vision.

- He visualized every day.
- He wrote his desire down clearly.
- He acted towards his dream without letting doubt win.

That's the Law of Attraction in action.

So today, ask yourself:

- What is YOUR $10 million dream?
- What vision are YOU holding on to?
- Are you thinking, acting and believing like the person who already has it?

If not, start now. Write it down. See it. Feel it. Act towards it.

Because if Jim Carrey could do it, so can you.

Day 34

The Power of Focus—Where Are You Looking?

Imagine standing at the edge of a river with a boat beside you. On the other side lies everything you desire—success, happiness, fulfilment. But between you and your dreams is the flowing water of life's uncertainties, setbacks and challenges.

Now, you have two choices:

A. You can stand at the edge, staring at the water, complaining about how strong the current is, how deep the river might be and how unfair it is that you have to cross it.

B. Or, you can step into the boat, pick up the oars and start rowing—focusing only on what you can control.

This is the power of focus. And the choice is always yours.

Choice 1: Focusing on what you CAN'T control

Most people unknowingly spend their entire lives fixated on things they have no power over.

- The economy is bad.
- People don't appreciate my efforts.
- My circumstances aren't ideal.
- The competition is too strong.

What happens when you focus on these things?

- You feel helpless.
- You become stuck in blame and excuses.
- You develop a victim mindset.
- You delay action because you believe external forces are stopping you.

The more you focus on things outside your control, the less energy you have to take action on things within your control.

Choice 2: Focusing on what you CAN control. Now, let's flip the perspective.

Instead of worrying about how bad the situation is, ask:

1. What CAN I do right now to improve my situation?
2. How can I adapt to this challenge instead of resisting it?
3. What small actions can I take today that bring me closer to my goal?

When you focus on what you can control, everything changes:

- You feel empowered.
- You take action instead of wasting time complaining.
- You attract more opportunities because you are actively working towards solutions.

Think about two students preparing for an exam:

✘ Student A spends hours stressing about how tough the syllabus is, how unfair the exam format is, and how the questions might be too difficult.

☑ Student B spends the same hours studying, revising, practising questions and preparing his mind for success.

Who do you think will perform better? This is why focus is the secret weapon of successful people.

- If you focus on why something won't work, the Universe gives you more obstacles.
- If you focus on what you can do today, the Universe aligns more opportunities for you.

The Universe rewards action, not excuses. So, ask yourself today:

- Where is my focus going?
- Am I focusing on the barriers, or am I looking for solutions?

- What small step can I take today towards my goals?

Remember, your life moves in the direction of your focus. Choose wisely.

Day 35

Aligning Your Beliefs with Your Desires

Let's start today with a little challenge.

Without using a calculator, answer this question as fast as you can:

A bat and a ball cost Rs 110 in total. The bat costs Rs 100 more than the ball.

How much does the ball cost?

Think about it for a moment. Your first instinct might say Rs 10. But is that really correct?

Let's break it down:

- If the ball costs Rs 10, and the bat is Rs 100 more, then the bat would be Rs 110.
- That makes the total Rs 120, not Rs 110.

The correct answer? The ball costs Rs 5, and the bat costs Rs 105.

Most people get this wrong—not because they don't know maths, but because their mind has been conditioned to take shortcuts and believe the first answer that *feels* right.

This brings us to today's lesson: *your beliefs shape your reality.*

But what actually happens when our beliefs are not aligned with our desires?

Imagine wanting to be rich, but deep down, you believe:

- *Money is hard to earn.*
- *Rich people are greedy.*
- *I don't deserve financial abundance.*

Now, ask yourself: if you subconsciously believe these things, will money ever flow into your life?

The truth is you cannot manifest what you do not believe in.

You may say *I want to be rich*. But if your mind is saying *I don't deserve wealth*, the Law of Attraction will not work in your favour.

This is why alignment of beliefs with desires is crucial.

But how does your inner world shape your outer world?

- If you believe you can be healthy, you will take actions that align with that belief—exercising, eating right and making better choices.
- If you believe you are confident, you will naturally speak and act with assurance.
- If you believe you are worthy of success, you will chase opportunities without hesitation.

But the moment your beliefs contradict your desires, you create resistance.

It's like trying to drive a car while stepping on the brakes. No matter how hard you push the accelerator, you won't move forward.

Now the question is, how to align beliefs with desires?

Step 1: Identify limiting beliefs.

Think about something you want. Now ask yourself:

- *Do I truly believe I can have it?*
- *What thoughts do I have about this goal?*
- *Are there any fears or doubts stopping me?*

Step 2: Rewire your mindset.

Once you find a limiting belief, flip it.

- Instead of *Money is hard to earn*, say *Money flows to me easily and effortlessly.*
- Instead of *I don't deserve success*, say *I am worthy of all the success I desire.*

Step 3: Act as if it's already yours.

- If you want wealth, start handling your current money with respect and gratitude.
- If you want confidence, practise speaking and walking with self-assurance.
- If you want love, treat yourself with kindness first.

The Universe doesn't respond to what you say—it responds to what you believe and embody.

Today, take a few moments to reflect:

- What do I want?
- Do I truly believe I can have it?
- If not, what belief do I need to change?

Because the moment your beliefs and desires align, the Universe has no choice but to deliver.

Day 36

The People Around
You Shape Your Destiny

Take a moment and think about the five people you interact with the most.

It could be your family, your friends, your colleagues or anyone you spend significant time with.

Now, ask yourself: *Are these people lifting me up or pulling me down?*

Because here's the truth:

'You are the average of the five people you spend the most time with.'

—Jim Rohn

If you constantly surround yourself with positive, driven and successful individuals, their energy and mindset will influence you to grow.

But if you spend time with negative, toxic or unmotivated people, you will inevitably start absorbing their energy.

There is a famous saying that goes:

'If you sit with four fools, the fifth fool is you. If you sit with four wise men, the fifth wise man is you.'

This wisdom is reflected in ancient Hindu philosophy as well:

संगत का असर अटल होता है, जैसे हवा जिस दिशा में चलती है, वह वातावरण को वैसा ही बना देती है।

The company you keep has a lasting effect, just like the wind shapes the environment around it.

Even the Bhagavad Gita (2.70) teaches that our thoughts, actions and ultimately our fate are shaped by those we associate with.

This means:

- If you spend time with inspired and hard-working individuals, you will naturally absorb their motivation.
- If you are surrounded by complainers and negative thinkers, you will subconsciously start adopting their mindset.

What happens when you are surrounded by negative people?

- *They drain your energy.* They always complain, criticize or see the worst in every situation.
- *They limit your growth.* They discourage you from chasing big goals because they don't believe in them.

- *They reinforce doubt.* If people around you don't believe in success, you will start doubting yourself too.

It's like being stuck in a room full of smoke; no matter how fresh the air outside is, you will start suffocating if you stay too long.

Now, let's flip the scenario. Imagine spending most of your time with:

1. *Optimistic, ambitious people*—they inspire you to take action.
2. *Solution-oriented thinkers*—they help you see opportunities instead of obstacles.
3. *Grateful and mindful individuals*—they uplift your energy and strengthen your mindset.

Their words and actions become a mirror for your own mindset.

Chanakya Niti (Chapter 1, Verse 8) states:

सर्पात् विप्रोऽपि दुर्युक्तः सर्पः तु दशति कालेन |
दुर्जनस्तु प्रदशति काले काले पुनः पुनः ||

Stay away from those who always see faults in everything. A snake bite is less dangerous than the poison of bad company.

This means that negative people not only impact your mind but also block your success.

But how to apply this in your own life?

1. Identify the top five people you spend time with.

____

____

____

____

2. Assess their influence—do they *inspire* or *drain* you?
3. *Minimize interaction with negative people.* If you can't avoid them completely, limit your exposure.
4. *Find new, positive influences.* Read books, listen to motivational speakers, and follow people who uplift you.

If you cannot find a positive circle yet, become your own source of positivity. Read, learn and grow until you attract the right people into your life.

Today, take a moment and reflect:

1. Are my closest connections shaping me into the person I want to become?
2. Do I need to make changes in my social environment?

Because your future is a reflection of the people you surround yourself with today. Choose wisely.

Day 37

Forgive, Release and Move On

Who is the one person you think you can never forgive in life?

Take a moment and think. Whose actions still hurt you? Who has wronged you so deeply that the very thought of them brings a wave of anger, sadness or resentment?

Now, I have something to say to you:

Forgive them.

I know this might feel impossible. You may be thinking *How can I forgive someone who caused me pain? They don't deserve my forgiveness.*

But today, I want you to understand why forgiveness is not for them—it is for you.

Holding on to resentment is like carrying a heavy suitcase everywhere you go. You may not see it, but it slows you down, tires you out and makes your journey unnecessarily difficult.

Imagine trying to climb a mountain, but you refuse to let go of a backpack full of rocks. Each rock represents anger, pain and bitterness. Now tell me, how far do you think you can climb with that weight on your back?

This is exactly what happens when you hold onto past grudges.

- *It drains your energy*. Your mind is constantly occupied by past wounds instead of focusing on the present and future.
- *It keeps you emotionally stuck*. You are stuck in a past situation that no longer exists, while life moves forward.
- *It blocks the flow of positivity*. The more you hold on to negativity, the harder it becomes for you to attract joy, success and love.

One of the biggest secrets of the Law of Attraction is that your energy attracts your reality. If you are constantly carrying negative emotions, the Universe will reflect that negativity back to you.

Let's make something clear:

1. Forgiving does not mean forgetting.
2. Forgiving does not mean excusing bad behaviour.
3. Forgiving does not mean allowing that person back into your life.

Forgiveness means releasing yourself from the chains of pain.

- You are not saying what they did was right.

- You are not allowing them to hurt you again.

You are simply saying *I will not let this person control my emotions anymore*.

Think about it—why should they continue to have power over your thoughts and feelings? Why should their actions of the past ruin your future?

When you forgive, you set yourself free.

Even science proves that forgiveness is beneficial:

- A study by the American Psychological Association found that people who practise forgiveness have lower blood pressure, reduced stress levels and a healthier heart.[12]
- Neuroscientists have discovered that holding on to anger activates the amygdala—the brain's stress centre—keeping you in a constant state of anxiety.[13]
- On the other hand, forgiveness activates the prefrontal cortex, which is linked to rational thinking, peace and emotional balance.

In simple terms, the more you forgive, the healthier and happier you become.

If you're ready to let go of this weight, here's how you can start:

1. Write a letter (but don't send it)
- Write to the person who hurt you. Express everything you feel.
- Then, burn or tear the letter as a symbolic way of releasing the pain.

2. Use the Ho'oponopono Technique
•   This ancient Hawaiian practice of forgiveness is simple yet powerful.
•   Close your eyes and repeat:
        I'm sorry.
        Please forgive me.
        Thank you.
        I love you.

3. Visualize yourself letting go
•   Imagine holding a balloon in your hands. That balloon represents the pain.
•   Now, in your mind, release it. Watch it float away.
•   Feel the weight lifting off your shoulders.

4. Shift your focus to gratitude
•   Instead of focusing on past pain, focus on the blessings in your life.
•   The more gratitude you practise, the less space resentment has to grow.

The Law of Attraction works best when your heart is light and your mind is clear. Holding on to anger blocks your blessings. Letting go opens new doors of abundance.

Today, take a deep breath and say:

1. *I choose to release the past.*
2. *I choose to free myself from negativity.*
3. *I choose peace.*

Because the lighter your heart, the higher you can fly.

Day 38

A Letter from the Future—Lady Gaga's Manifestation Secret

Imagine waking up one day feeling lost and uncertain about your future, wondering if your dreams will ever come true.

Now, imagine receiving a letter, written by you, but from the future. A version of yourself who has already achieved everything you desire.

Wouldn't that be powerful?

Before Lady Gaga became a global superstar, she was just another struggling artist, trying to make her mark in the music industry.

At one point in her life, she wrote herself a letter—one that spoke as if her success had already happened.

In that letter, she told herself:

'I have fans all over the world. My songs are loved. I am living my dream.'

She wasn't just wishing; she was declaring it as reality. She wrote with conviction, as if she had already become the artist she dreamed of being.

Fast forward a few years, and everything in that letter became true.

This is the power of future self-communication.

1. *It shifts your mindset.* Writing as your successful future self makes you start thinking, acting and believing like that person today.
2. *It creates emotional alignment.* When you deeply feel the reality of your future self, the Universe responds by aligning your path to that outcome.
3. *It helps you stay focused.* Reading your future self's words keeps you on track, even when challenges arise.

Think about it: if your future self already knows you've made it, why would you doubt yourself now?

So, here's your task for today: take a piece of paper and a pen and write a letter from your future self to your present self.

Start with

📝 *Dear [Your Name], I am so proud of you! You have achieved . . .*

Describe your success as if it has already happened:

- Where you live.
- What your daily life looks like.
- What you've achieved.
- How you feel.

Sign off as your future self, who already knows you're going to make it.

Now, seal the letter away or set a reminder to read it in a month. Let the magic unfold.

Lady Gaga didn't just dream; she declared her future into existence. And so can you.

Believe it. Write it. Live it.

Because the future 'you' is already waiting—you just have to step into it.

Day 39

Move Your Body,
Elevate Your Energy

Imagine waking up feeling sluggish, unmotivated and a little lost. You try to shake it off, maybe by scrolling through your phone or making a cup of coffee, but the feeling lingers.

Now, recall a time when you took a walk outside, played a sport, danced or simply stretched your body. Did you notice how your mood lifted almost instantly? This is because movement generates energy, and energy shapes your vibrations.

Every *thought*, *action* and *emotion* carries a vibrational frequency. The higher your vibration, the more positive energy you radiate, and the more aligned you become with success, joy and abundance.

When you feel *stuck*, *exhausted* or *uninspired*, it's often a sign of low vibrational energy. But the best way to reset and elevate your vibration is by engaging in physical activities that uplift your spirit.

Why does this happen? Because your mind and body are deeply connected. When you move, your body releases endorphins, dopamine and serotonin—the chemicals responsible for happiness, motivation and focus.

The Law of Attraction states that you attract what you focus on and feel. When your body feels energized and positive, your thoughts follow the same pattern. Physical movement helps create the right mindset and emotional state to attract your goals.

Let's explore how different physical activities can help boost your energy and vibrations:

1. **Walking in nature.** Spending time in nature is one of the easiest ways to reset your energy levels. Walking outside, breathing fresh air and feeling the warmth of the sun reduces stress, enhances creativity and brings mental clarity. Research suggests that just twenty minutes in a natural setting can lower cortisol levels, the hormone responsible for stress.

2. **Running or swimming.** These activities create a steady rhythm that clears your mind. When you engage in cardio-based activities, your heart rate increases, sending more oxygen to your brain, improving focus and elevating your mood. Studies show that people who exercise regularly experience higher levels of confidence and resilience.

3. **Dancing or playing a sport.** Movement through dancing or competitive sports allows you to express yourself freely. The energy of engagement, play and joy lifts your frequency, bringing spontaneous moments of happiness and clarity. Many high achievers, from

entrepreneurs to artists, swear by regular physical activity as a way to maintain a high-energy mindset.

4. **Yoga and stretching.** Yoga is more than just physical exercise. It aligns your breath, body, and mind, helping you enter a flow state where negative thoughts dissolve. Stretching in the morning or before bed can help release tension, improve flexibility and create a sense of calm.

Numerous studies back up the idea that physical movement is essential for mental well-being and energy alignment.

- Harvard Medical School research states that just ten minutes of exercise can boost cognitive function, improve problem-solving skills and enhance overall mood.[14]
- A study found that exercise increases neuroplasticity, meaning your brain becomes more adaptable and open to new opportunities.[15]
- Psychologists agree that people who move their bodies regularly experience lower stress levels, increased motivation and a stronger sense of purpose.[16]

This means that the more you move, the easier it becomes to maintain a high-energy, goal-focused mindset.

Today, take at least twenty minutes to engage in a physical activity that resonates with you.

- Go for a walk in the fresh air.
- Do a light stretching session.

- Play your favourite song and dance freely.
- Try a short run, a swim or a fun sport.

As you move, pay attention to how your energy shifts. Observe how your thoughts become clearer, your emotions lighter and your motivation stronger. If possible, make this a daily practice and notice how it transforms not only your mindset but also your ability to attract what you desire.

Your physical state directly impacts your mental and emotional state. When you take care of your body, you automatically raise your energy levels and invite more positivity into your life.

- The more you move, the more energy you create.
- The more energy you create, the higher your vibrations rise.
- The higher your vibrations, the faster you attract abundance.

Start moving today and let your energy work for you.

Day 40

The Power of Your Environment

Take a moment to look around your surroundings. What do you see? Is your space clean, organized and inviting? Or is it cluttered, messy and overwhelming?

Now, imagine stepping into a beautifully arranged, well-lit room, where everything is in its place and there's fresh air flowing through the windows. How does it make you feel?

Compare that to stepping into a chaotic, cluttered room filled with scattered papers, dusty shelves and dim lighting. Does it feel draining?

This is the power of your environment—it directly impacts your thoughts, energy and ability to manifest.

The Law of Attraction teaches us that our outer world is a reflection of our inner world.

If your space is cluttered, chaotic and dark, it subconsciously creates feelings of stress, confusion and stagnation. But when your space is clean, open and bright, it allows positivity, clarity and inspiration to flow freely.

Think about it: when was the last time you deep-cleaned your room or reorganized your desk? Didn't you feel a sense of relief, accomplishment and fresh energy afterward?

Your physical space shapes your mental space.

- A messy environment can make you feel stuck, unmotivated and distracted.
- A clean and decluttered space invites fresh opportunities, new ideas and mental clarity.

Decluttering isn't just about cleaning your house; it's about clearing out old, stagnant energy to make room for new possibilities.

Many ancient traditions, including Vastu Shastra and Feng Shui, emphasize the importance of an uncluttered space for attracting prosperity and positive energy.

Here's how decluttering affects your energy:

- *Removes stagnant energy*. Clutter holds onto past emotions, unfinished tasks and stress. Letting go of old items clears this trapped energy.
- *Increases focus and productivity*. A clean, organized space makes it easier to concentrate, think clearly and feel motivated.
- *Boosts your mood*. Research shows that a clutter-free environment reduces stress and anxiety, making you feel lighter and more in control.
- *Invites new opportunities*. The Universe loves open spaces. When you remove unnecessary items, you

symbolically show the Universe you're ready to receive new things.

Ask yourself:

- *Do I have items I no longer use or need?*
- *Are there broken things in my space that I haven't fixed or discarded?*
- *Does my environment make me feel energized or drained?*

If your space feels overwhelming, it's time to declutter.

Light plays a huge role in shaping your mood, energy and vibrations.

A dark, poorly lit space can make you feel tired, sluggish and uninspired. In contrast, a well-lit, airy space can uplift your mood, sharpen your focus, and boost creativity.

Here's what you can do to optimize your space for positive energy:

1. *Let natural light in.* Open your curtains during the day to invite sunlight, which is known to increase happiness and reduce stress.
2. *Use warm, bright lights in work areas.* If natural light isn't available, ensure your workspace has adequate lighting to keep you focused and alert.
3. *Bring in fresh air.* Open windows or use air-purifying plants like snake plants or peace lilies to maintain clean, breathable air.

These simple changes can have a profound effect on your daily mood and energy levels. Take twenty minutes today and declutter a small area in your environment.

- *Start with one space*. Your desk, wardrobe or a corner of your room.
- *Remove unnecessary items*. If you haven't used something in the last six months, ask yourself if you truly need it.
- *Clean and reorganize*. Wipe down surfaces, neatly arrange your items and ensure the area feels open and welcoming.
- *Let in fresh air and light*. Open the windows and let new energy flow in.

Once you're done, observe how your energy shifts.

Do you feel lighter? More at ease? More motivated?

Your environment is not just a reflection of your current state—it's a powerful tool for shaping your future.

- A clutter-free space invites clarity and peace.
- A bright, fresh environment attracts abundance.
- A well-organized space helps you stay focused on your goals.

Start curating your surroundings with intention, and watch how it transforms your energy, mindset and ability to manifest everything you desire.

Day 41

Sharma Ji Ka Beta—Your Success, Your Timeline

Let's start with a brain teaser:

What is the most common phrase heard in all Indian households during dinner time?

Think for a second.

Got it? Here's the answer:

Sharma ji ka beta dekh kaha place ho gaya, aur tum kya karne wale ho life mai?

Look at how successful Sharma ji's son is, and where are you?

Sounds familiar, doesn't it?

Every household has a 'Sharma ji ka beta'—the gold standard of success, the one everyone is compared to. But let's flip the script.

Sharma ji ka beta . . . Sharma ji ka beta hai. Main, main hoon. Mujhe jab success milegi tab milegi.

Now, why is this important? Because the biggest mistake we make in life is comparing our journey with someone else's.

We live in a world where social media, family expectations and peer pressure make us feel that if we don't achieve success early, we are 'failing'.

- If someone gets their dream job at twenty-five, does that mean you can't get it at thirty?
- If someone buys a house at twenty-eight, does that mean you can't buy yours at thirty-five?
- If someone starts a business at twenty-two and makes millions, does that mean your entrepreneurial journey at forty is useless?

Absolutely not.

Your timeline is your own. Your path is different, your challenges are different and your journey is not meant to look like someone else's.

Imagine a marathon—some runners finish in two hours, some in four hours, but does that mean those who take longer haven't completed the race? No. They still cross the finish line and achieve what they set out to do.

It's good to look at successful people for inspiration, not comparison. There's a big difference between learning from someone and using their achievements as a reason to doubt yourself.

Ask yourself:

1. *Am I feeling inspired by their story, or am I feeling inadequate?*

2. *Am I using their success as motivation, or am I using it to beat myself up?*
3. *What actions can I take to create my own success instead of focusing on theirs?*

You should always take inspiration from the success of others, but walk your own path to create your own version of it.

Take action on your own journey

Instead of worrying about how far ahead someone else is, focus on what you can do today.

- If someone got a great job, work on improving your skills, resume and opportunities.
- If someone started a business, research, plan and take small steps towards yours.
- If someone achieved financial stability, start working on your savings and investments.

Every step counts. The Law of Attraction doesn't work by simply wishing; it works when you align your thoughts with actions.

Harland Sanders, famously known as 'Colonel Sanders', didn't achieve success until he was sixty-five. After facing multiple failures in jobs and businesses and even getting rejected over 1000 times while pitching his fried chicken recipe, he finally built KFC into a global brand. Imagine if he had compared himself to young entrepreneurs and given up; KFC wouldn't exist today. His story is proof that success has no age limit, and your timeline is uniquely yours.

If you keep looking at someone else's life, you will miss the opportunities in your own.

To end today's lesson, here's a powerful Sanskrit shloka:

स्वधर्मे निधनं श्रेयः परधर्मो भयावहः

It is better to fail in your own path than to succeed in someone else's.

I won't explain this to you. Take a moment, reflect on it and find your own meaning in these words.

Day 42

The Mistake That Stops Manifestation—Doubting the Process

Before we begin today, let's check in on your progress.

I want you to pause for a moment and reflect on everything we've practised so far. Take a pencil and tick off the techniques you have been following consistently:

- ☐ Daily affirmations
- ☐ Visualization
- ☐ Gratitude practice
- ☐ Meditative techniques
- ☐ Law of Attraction exercises (3-6-9, 5x55, water technique, etc.)
- ☐ Taking aligned actions towards your goals

Now, look at your checkmarks. How many did you tick? Are there any practices you have missed or done inconsistently?

Take a moment to acknowledge your progress, but also be honest with yourself.

Have you ever had thoughts like these?

- *I have been manifesting for twenty days, and I see no results.*
- *I've been practising the Law of Attraction for three months, but nothing has happened.*
- *I've been working with the Law of Attraction for five years, and I'm still waiting.*

If you've had even a single thought like this, then you've already made the one mistake that is blocking your manifestation.

You are doubting the process.

The biggest reason people fail with the Law of Attraction is because they lose trust in divine timing.

They start with enthusiasm, confidence and belief. But as time passes and their desires don't manifest instantly, they start to feel impatient, frustrated or even desperate.

And here's the truth:

If you doubt, you delay. If you quit, you block.

Manifestation isn't about demanding things from the Universe. It's about aligning yourself with the right energy, timing and actions to receive what's meant for you.

If you feel like nothing is happening, ask yourself these three questions:

1. *Is my desire large, and does it require more effort?*

Some manifestations require more time, alignment and work.

- Wanting a cup of coffee? You might get it in minutes.
- Manifesting your dream career? It might take months or years of personal growth, learning and action.
- Attracting your soulmate? The Universe may need to arrange a sequence of events to bring you together at the right time.

Some things require time to unfold. Instead of questioning the delay, trust that everything is aligning behind the scenes.

2. *Am I truly aligned, or do I have hidden doubts?*

If you've been practising, but nothing is happening, check whether you have deeply buried doubts.

- Do you secretly think *This won't work for me*?
- Do you feel *I don't deserve this*?
- Are you afraid of success or change?

Even the smallest subconscious doubt can act as a block. The solution? Reinforce belief. Keep affirming, visualizing and aligning your thoughts with certainty.

3. *Am I acting out of desperation?*

When people desperately want something, they put out an energy of lack.

- *I need this now!* Sends a signal of urgency and impatience.
- *Why isn't it here yet?* Sends a signal of frustration and lack.

The Universe does not respond well to desperation. It works on abundance and trust.

If you're feeling restless or impatient, take a step back. Focus on becoming the person who naturally attracts what you desire, instead of chasing after it.

If you realize you've been making any of these mistakes, here's what I want you to do:

- Restart this book (or your Law of Attraction journey) with your new understanding.
- Identify what you may have been missing—belief, patience or consistency.
- Trust the Universe's timing—you will receive your desire when it is meant for you.
- Stay consistent—the Law of Attraction works for those who stay in alignment, no matter how long it takes.

The Universe or God will always give you what you want—but only when the time is right.

Your only job is to keep believing, keep working, and stay aligned.

Don't plant a seed and keep digging it up to check if it's growing. Water it, nurture it and trust that it will bloom.

Day 43

Dream Diary—A Portable
Vision Board

Before we begin today, let me ask you something:

Have you made your vision board yet?

If your answer is YES, great! You are already on the right path.

If your answer is NO, then I want you to pause and rethink your approach. After today's discussion, you'll see why having a physical representation of your dreams is so important.

And if you haven't made one yet, your homework for today is to make it before tomorrow.

Now, let's talk about an alternative for those who might struggle with a vision board:

The Dream Diary

A dream diary works just like a vision board, but instead of putting everything on a board, you write it down in a diary.

This diary becomes your personalized space where you:

- Buy a diary, preferably with yellow pages and a red/green pen.
- Write down your dreams and goals.
- Paste pictures related to them (similar to a vision board).
- Write notes, emotions, affirmations and thoughts related to your desires.

It's your own private space where your dreams come alive in words and images.

And most importantly:

You should open this diary once per day and read through it, just like you would look at a vision board.

Vision boards are a fantastic tool, but they are meant to be displayed in an open space. However, not everyone has that luxury or comfort.

A dream diary is perfect for:

- People living in college hostels or dorms who don't have personal space to display a vision board.
- People who are shy or introverted and don't feel comfortable displaying their dreams openly.
- People who travel frequently and need a portable way to keep their vision aligned with their goals.

If you resonate with any of the above, then a dream diary might be the right choice for you.

Dream diary vs vision board—what's the difference?

While both the vision board and dream diary help you manifest your dreams, they cater to different personalities and situations. Here's a structured breakdown of how they differ:

- Vision board:
  o Relies primarily on visual representation (pictures, symbols and images).
  o Needs to be displayed somewhere visible (like a bedroom wall or workspace).
  o Helps you reinforce your dreams through daily visual engagement.
  o Best suited for people who like constant reminders and enjoy seeing their goals in front of them.

- Dream diary:
  o Combines written affirmations and visual elements (pictures + notes).
  o Meant to be private and personal; no need for public display.
  o Helps in detailed goal-setting and emotional connection through writing.
  o Ideal for people who prefer introspection, privacy or a lack of personal space for a vision board.

But how do we choose which to choose?

- If you are comfortable displaying your goals and enjoy visual motivation, a vision board is your best choice.

- If you prefer keeping your dreams personal or want more written reflection, a dream diary is better suited.

No matter which one you pick, consistency is key. Make sure to engage with it daily!

One of my students always struggled with visualization. She told me, 'Sir, I love the idea of a vision board, but I live in a shared hostel. I can't display my dreams for everyone to see.'

I suggested she try the dream diary instead—writing down her goals daily, adding small pictures and describing how she would feel once they came true. She committed to it, reading and writing in her diary every morning and night.

A few months later, she sent me a message: 'It's working! My first diary is all checked out, and now I'm working with a new one!'

Her success wasn't luck. It was clarity, consistency, and belief. Whether it's a vision board or a dream diary, what matters is engaging with your dreams daily. Because when you write them down, the Universe takes notice.

Now that you know the importance of keeping your dreams in front of you, it's time to take action:

1. If you haven't made a vision board yet, start working on it today.
2. If you prefer privacy, create a dream diary instead.
3. Whichever method you choose, use it daily! Look at your vision board every morning or read through and write in your dream diary.

Your dreams deserve space in your life—make sure they have one!

Day 44

Understanding Your Energy—Is It Positive or Negative?

Alright, tell me something:

How are you feeling right now?

Take a deep breath, close your eyes for a few seconds and truly check in with yourself. What emotions are running through your mind? Are you feeling relaxed, happy and excited? Or are you feeling tired, overwhelmed or distracted?

Now, let's start with a simple exercise to centre ourselves:

1. Look around and pick three things that you are grateful for.
2. Hold on to those thoughts for a moment and appreciate them.
3. Smile and remind yourself that you are blessed in many ways.

Now, take a moment to reflect on the emotions you just experienced. How do you feel? Has anything shifted?

This brings us to today's discussion:

Understanding Your Energy.

The energy we carry influences every single aspect of our lives, including how well the Law of Attraction works for us. If our energy is positive, we attract opportunities, success and happiness. If it is negative, we push away the things we desire.

Let's break this down:

1. Positive energy

- You feel happy, calm and collected.
- You are focused and know what you need to do.
- You feel motivated and confident about your goals.
- You are proactive, taking steps to improve your life.
- Your mind is clear, and you feel at peace.
- You wake up feeling excited for the day and ready to take action.

2. Negative energy

- You feel lethargic, distracted or unmotivated.
- You have self-doubt and question your abilities.
- You feel agitated, frustrated or overwhelmed.
- You struggle to focus and feel lost.
- Your thoughts are chaotic, making it hard to take action.

- You wake up feeling drained or unwilling to start the day.

A person carrying negative energy often feels stuck. No matter how much they try, things don't seem to work out because their energy is not aligned with their desires. But the good news is that energy is fluid, and it can change.

If you feel like you are carrying negative energy, don't worry—it can be changed! The key is to engage in activities that uplift your spirit and bring you joy.

Here are some ways to shift your energy:

- *Do what you love*. Whether it's painting, dancing, reading or listening to music, doing things you genuinely enjoy boosts your energy instantly.
- *Exercise and move your body*. Physical activity, even something as simple as stretching or walking, releases endorphins that help shift your mood and energy. Studies show that just twenty minutes of moderate exercise can improve mood and increase productivity.
- *Surround yourself with positivity*. Spend time with people who uplift and inspire you rather than those who drain you. There is a saying: *'If you spend time with five motivated people, you will become the sixth. If you spend time with five complainers, you will also become the sixth.'*
- *Practise gratitude daily*. The simple act of acknowledging what you are grateful for can change your entire energy state. Gratitude activates the brain's reward system, increasing feelings of happiness and fulfilment.

- *Take action.* Sometimes, energy shifts the moment you start working towards your goals instead of overthinking them. Progress fuels positivity.
- *Declutter your space.* A messy environment often creates mental clutter. Cleaning up your space can help you feel mentally refreshed and emotionally lighter.
- *Watch your words.* What you say to yourself matters. Instead of saying '*I am stuck*', try '*I am finding a way forward*'. Words influence our subconscious, which in turn affects our energy.

Take a moment now to assess your current energy level. What kind of energy are you carrying today? If it's positive, keep nurturing it. If it's negative, choose one of the methods above and take a small step towards shifting it.

Remember: Your energy shapes your reality. The more positive and aligned it is, the closer you get to manifesting your dreams. Make the choice today to uplift your energy and watch how your life starts changing!

Day 45

The Power of Perspective—Half Empty or Half Full?

Okay, let's see if you can answer this one. Read this carefully and think before you answer:

You are in a dark room with a single candle, a matchbox and a lantern. You need to light up the room. What do you light first?

Think carefully.

Got your answer?

Most people say the candle or the lantern . . . but do you know what the correct answer is? It is the *matchstick!*

This is a perfect example of how we often overlook the obvious and focus on the wrong details.

You have probably heard the famous analogy– *a glass filled to 50 per cent capacity can be seen in two ways:*

- Half-empty: focusing on what's missing.
- Half-full: focusing on what's still there.

This simple analogy is a mirror to our mindset in life.

1. The half-empty mindset:

- Focuses on what is lacking rather than what is present.
- Leads to complaints, negativity, and disappointment.
- Creates an attitude of scarcity, making it difficult to attract abundance.

2. The half-full mindset:

- Focuses on what is available rather than what is missing.
- Leads to gratitude, positivity and motivation.
- Helps develop an abundance mindset, attracting more opportunities.

If you always look at the empty part of the glass, you will never feel satisfied or happy. But if you start seeing the full part of the glass, you will begin to attract more positivity, growth and abundance into your life.

Here's an example to think about:

- You want to start a business, but you don't have enough capital. Do you:
  - **A:** Complain about not having enough money and give up?
  - **B:** Look for what resources you do have and find ways to start small?

- You didn't get selected for a job interview. Do you:
  - o **A:** Feel like a failure and assume you will never get a job?
  - o **B:** Learn from the experience, improve your skills and apply again?

See the pattern? Your perspective shapes your reality.

The Law of Attraction is deeply connected to how you view your life. If you keep focusing on what's missing and constantly feeling bad about it, you are sending signals of scarcity to the Universe. As a result, you will attract more scarcity.

But if you focus on what you already have, you are telling the Universe:

I appreciate what I have, and I am ready for more!

And guess what? The Universe responds to this energy by bringing you more of what you focus on!

Now that you understand the power of perspective, let's practise it:

1. Write down three things in your life that you feel are lacking.
2. Reframe each one to focus on the positive side instead of the negative.
3. Read them out loud and feel the shift in energy.

Here's an example:

- *Negative Thought:* I don't have my dream job yet.
- *Positive Reframe:* I am learning and improving every day to get closer to my dream job.

Starting today, make it a habit to focus on what's full in your glass rather than what's empty. The more you train your mind to see the positives, the more abundance, success and happiness you will attract.

Your life is already filled with so many blessings— you just have to choose to see them!

Day 46

The Secret to Attracting Your Own Success

Today I want to ask you a very important question. And I want you to answer it honestly.

Think about the last time a friend of yours got promoted or achieved something big.

How did you feel?

Did you genuinely feel happy for them and congratulate them with a full heart? If so, then congratulations—you already understand today's lesson!

But if you had thoughts like

- *Why didn't I get that promotion?*
- *What is so special about them?*
- *Why not me?*

Then you need to stay with me because **this discussion might change how you attract success in your life.**

When we see someone else succeeding, it's easy to feel envy, frustration or self-doubt. It's a natural reaction, but what happens when we feel this way?

Here's what actually happens on an energy level:

⬤ **If you feel jealous or upset when someone succeeds**

- You are sending signals to the Universe that success makes you unhappy.
- The Universe, being neutral, doesn't judge—it only reflects your emotions back to you.
- Seeing your negative response to success, the Universe assumes that success is something you don't like, and, therefore, it stops sending it your way.

⬤ **If you feel happy and celebrate other people's success**

- You are telling the Universe that success is something you welcome.
- Your emotions create an abundant energy field that attracts more success to you.
- The Universe sees that success makes you happy, so it sends more success your way.

This is one of the biggest mistakes people make when using the Law of Attraction. They unknowingly block their own blessings by reacting negatively to others' achievements.

The Universe doesn't give you what you want; it gives you what you are aligned with. If you constantly feel bitter or jealous when others win, you are aligning yourself with lack, disappointment and scarcity.

But when you genuinely feel happy for others, your energy shifts to gratitude, positivity and abundance. And as we have learnt, what you put out is what you receive.

This is why some people seem to attract opportunities effortlessly; they celebrate success, no matter whose it is.

Next time someone around you achieves something great, catch your reaction.

If jealousy or resentment comes up, pause and reframe your thoughts.

Instead of thinking

⬤ *Why not me?*

Think

⬤ *This means success is possible! If they can do it, I can too.*

Instead of thinking

⬤ *They don't deserve it.*

Think

⬤ *Their journey is different from mine. My time is coming.*

Warren Buffett, one of the world's greatest investors, has always been vocal about celebrating the success of others.

In his early years, when he saw Bill Gates revolutionizing the tech industry, he didn't feel threatened; he admired him. In fact, instead of competing, Buffett and Gates formed one of the most impactful friendships in business history.

Buffett has often stated that **success should not be seen as a limited resource**, and his attitude of admiration over competition has helped him build long-lasting, successful relationships. By celebrating others' achievements, he attracted even more opportunities and wealth into his own life.

Instead of feeling envious, use their success as proof that what you want is achievable.

1. Think of three people you know who have recently achieved something great.
2. Send them a message or call them to congratulate them with a full heart.
3. Write down one thing you admire about their journey. What can you learn from it?

By doing this, you are shifting your mindset from competition to inspiration, from scarcity to abundance.

A study published in the *Journal of Personality and Social Psychology* found that people who engage in 'positive reframing' when seeing others succeed—meaning they reinterpret envy as motivation—are significantly more likely to achieve their own goals.

The Law of Attraction works based on what you put out into the world. If you radiate jealousy and lack, you will receive more of the same. But if you radiate happiness and abundance for others, success will find its way to you too.

Remember, *the energy you send out is the energy that returns to you*. So, celebrate every success you see, because yours is on its way!

Day 47

Your Thoughts Today
Shape Your Future

Let's begin today with a powerful verse from the
Bhagavad Gita:

उद्धरेदात्मनात्मानं नात्मानमवसादयेत् ।
आत्मैव ह्यात्मनो बन्धुरात्मैव रिपुरात्मनः ॥

*One must elevate oneself by one's own mind and not
degrade oneself. The self alone is one's friend, and the
self alone is one's enemy.*

—Bhagavad Gita 6.5

This verse tells us that our mind is the ultimate creator of
our reality; it can either keep us trapped in struggles or
lead us towards success and freedom.

Now, let's reflect on a thought I always share with my viewers:

जो आप आज सोच रहे हैं, वही आपका कल बनेगा; जो आप कल सोचेंगे, वह आपका परसों बनेगा, तो अपने आज को ही सफल बना लेते हैं।

What you think today becomes your tomorrow. What you think tomorrow shapes your future. So why not make today successful?

This statement holds the core essence of the Law of Attraction—your present thoughts are shaping your future, moment by moment.

Think of your thoughts as seeds you plant in the soil of your mind. Every positive thought is a seed for success, and every negative thought is a seed for struggle. The more you nurture these thoughts, the more they grow into your reality.

If you constantly think

- *My life is tough. Nothing ever works out for me.*
- *I am not lucky enough to achieve success.*

Then your future will reflect those exact limitations.

But if you choose to think

- *I am learning, growing and getting closer to my goals every day.*
- *Success is already on its way to me.*

Then your future shapes itself towards abundance and opportunities.

- **Your mind acts like a magnet.**
  What you think about most often gets attracted into your life. Your subconscious starts working in that direction.

- **Your actions follow your thoughts.**
  If you think you are incapable, you won't take action. But if you believe in yourself, you'll find ways to move forward.

- **Your energy affects the universe.**
  Your thoughts carry vibrations. Positive thoughts attract positive situations, and negative thoughts repel them.

This is why success doesn't start with action—it starts with thinking like a successful person!

Many people live in their past struggles instead of focusing on a successful future. But here's the truth:

- Your past does not define you.
- Your future is not fixed; it is shaped by what you think and do today.

If you keep thinking about failures, you are unknowingly repeating them in the future. But if you focus on success, opportunities and growth, you create a future full of achievements.

Let's practise a simple exercise to train your mind for success:

1. Write down three thoughts you repeatedly have about your life.
2. If they are negative, reframe them into a positive version.
3. Repeat the positive thoughts to yourself five times today.

For example:

● Negative Thought: *I am always stuck in the same place.*
● Positive Thought: *Every day, I am growing and moving towards success.*

What you think and feel today is designing your future. If you want a successful tomorrow, start thinking and believing in success today.

From this moment forward, let's make a promise:

I will think, act and believe in my success, because my thoughts today will build my future!

Day 48

The Secret Tool to Keep You Motivated Anywhere, Anytime

Imagine this: you're having a tough day, things aren't going as planned and your energy is dropping. In moments like these, wouldn't it be great if you had a personal coach whispering words of encouragement directly to you?

Well, here's a simple life hack that does exactly that—**Affirmation Cards.**

Affirmation cards are small, credit card-sized pieces of paper that carry powerful affirmations you have written for yourself. They act as instant energy boosters whenever you feel low, distracted or in doubt. These cards remind you of your strength, goals and the positivity you are cultivating in life.

1. **Size Matters:** The cards should be small enough to fit into your wallet, purse or pocket—like a credit card or ID card.

2. **Personalized power:** You handwrite one to three affirmations that resonate deeply with you.

3. **Easy access:** Anytime you need a boost of motivation, take out a card, read the affirmations silently, absorb the energy and put it back.
4. **Choose your material:** You can use a cardboard cutout, an A4 sheet cut to size or any small sturdy paper.
5. **Write your affirmations:** Keep them short, powerful and specific. For example:
   o *I am confident and capable in everything I do.*
   o *Abundance flows easily into my life.*
   o *I attract success and happiness effortlessly.*

6. **Carry them with you:** Always keep your affirmation cards in your wallet or pocket for easy access.
7. **Use them when needed:** Whenever you feel low, lost or demotivated, pull out a card, read it, feel it, believe it and return it.

Want to understand what you can gain from doing these simple actions?

- **Instant energy boost:** Repeating affirmations shifts your mental state immediately.
- **Breaks negative loops:** When doubts creep in, reading your affirmations interrupts negative thought patterns.
- **Triggers positive action:** Seeing your affirmations reminds you to stay on track with your goals.
- **Constant reminder:** Unlike digital notes, physical affirmation cards engage your senses, making affirmations more impactful.

Many successful people use this method to stay focused, confident and positive in any situation. If you've ever felt the need for an instant recharge, this is your personal pocket-sized solution.

So, create your affirmation cards today and let them be your silent motivators!

Day 49

The Mistake That Slows Down
Your Manifestations

Alright, ROLL CALL! A quick self-check is what we are going to do first today. How have your daily Law of Attraction practices been going? Take a moment and mark the ones you have been consistently following:

- Daily affirmations
- Visualization
- Gratitude practice
- Meditation and energy work
- Manifestation exercises (vision board, dream diary, 3-6-9 method, etc.)

Now, pause for a second and ask yourself this:

What do I do immediately after completing my Law of Attraction practices?

Think about it. Do you go back to your usual routine, feeling inspired and full of positive energy? Or do you end up doing something that instantly drains that energy?

Here's a simple truth: what you do after your Law of Attraction practices is just as important as doing the practices themselves.

Many people dedicate ten to fifteen minutes every day to affirmations, visualization, gratitude or meditation, and then they unknowingly sabotage all that positive energy by engaging in negative, draining activities.

Want to see how? Try these simple exercises:

- You finish your morning affirmations, feeling confident and motivated. Then, you turn on the news and hear about a major financial crisis. Your energy immediately drops.

- You complete a powerful visualization session, but the moment you pick up your phone, someone calls with complaints, gossip or bad news, instantly shifting your mood.

- You finish scripting your goals, then start scrolling on social media, comparing yourself to others, feeling envious or unmotivated.

- You meditate and feel deeply at peace, but then you enter a heated argument with a family member or colleague, bringing stress and frustration back into your energy field.

What happened here? The ten to fifteen minutes of positive energy you created just got neutralized.

The Law of Attraction responds to your dominant vibration. If you start your day with high-energy affirmations but then expose yourself to negativity, your dominant energy shifts downward.

It's like lighting a candle and immediately blowing it out; it doesn't get a chance to shine.

Right after deep focus or visualization, your subconscious mind is highly impressionable. This means if you consume negative information immediately after your practice, your mind starts absorbing fear instead of faith.

A study in neuroscience suggests that the first twenty to thirty minutes after deep mental focus (like meditation or affirmations) is a golden period where your mind is more open to suggestions. If you fill this period with positive reinforcement, your subconscious locks in those beliefs. If you fill it with doubt, stress or negativity, your subconscious holds on to that instead.

Your manifestations don't just depend on one session of affirmations; they depend on how often you maintain that energy throughout the day.

If you affirm in the morning that you are attracting abundance, but for the rest of the day, you are complaining about money, which signal do you think the Universe will respond to?

Instead of draining your energy after your Law of Attraction practices, here's what you should do instead:

1. **Stay in the energy of positivity**
    After affirmations or visualization, stay mindful and enjoy that feeling. Let it linger for at least ten to fifteen minutes before engaging in daily tasks.

2. **Be selective with your environment**
    Avoid negative news, gossip, toxic conversations or stressful situations immediately after your practice. Protect your positive energy.

3. **Consume uplifting content**
    Listen to motivational podcasts, read an inspiring book or watch something that aligns with your goals. Fill your mind with content that supports your manifestation.

4. **Take actions aligned with your manifestation**
*   If you visualized a fit and healthy body, go for a walk or eat a healthy meal.
*   If you affirmed financial success, start working on a project that brings value.
*   If you meditated for inner peace, continue with activities that keep you calm.

5. **Set intentions for the rest of the day**
    Before moving on with your tasks, pause and affirm: *I am carrying this positive energy with me throughout the day. Everything I do aligns with my desires.*

If you've ever wondered why your manifestations are taking longer, this could be the reason. It's not just about doing Law of Attraction practices; it's about maintaining that energy throughout the day.

So, from today onwards, be mindful of what you do after your Law of Attraction sessions. The Universe is always responding to your energy—make sure it's the right one!

Day 50

The Ultimate Law of Attraction Morning Routine

Congratulations on reaching halfway through this journey! You have already come so far, and every step you take brings you closer to the life you desire. Keep moving forward, for persistence is the key to unlocking the magic of the Universe.

Today is special. You are at the fifty-day mark! That means you have spent the last forty-nine days practising, learning and growing with the Law of Attraction. You have built strong habits, overcome limiting beliefs and made progress in shifting your energy towards your desires.

But we are not stopping here! This is just the beginning. The next fifty days will be even more powerful because now you have experience, awareness, and clarity. You are no longer someone who *hopes* the Law of Attraction works; you are now someone who *knows* it works.

Over the past forty-nine days, we have covered multiple aspects of the Law of Attraction. Here's a quick recap of some of the key do's and don'ts we have discussed:

Dos

- **Practise gratitude daily:** The Universe rewards those who are thankful. The more gratitude you express, the more abundance you attract.
- **Stay consistent with your affirmations:** Repeating affirmations regularly conditions your subconscious mind for success.
- **Visualize with emotion:** The stronger the emotions behind your visualization, the faster you manifest your goals.
- **Take action:** Manifestation doesn't work without action. The Universe provides opportunities, but it is your job to act on them.
- **Surround yourself with positive energy:** Whether it's through people, environments, or thoughts, positivity fuels manifestation.

Don'ts

- **Doubt the process:** The biggest mistake people make is questioning *when* their manifestation will happen. This delays the process.
- **Obsess over the outcome:** You must let go and trust the Universe's timing. Desperation blocks attraction.
- **Engage in negative self-talk:** What you say and think about yourself becomes your reality.

- **Neglect physical and mental well-being:** Your energy is affected by your lifestyle. If your mind and body are unhealthy, it slows down your manifestation.

Now that we have reinforced these learnings, let's start today's exercise and set the tone for the ultimate Law of Attraction morning routine.

Before we move forward, let's take a moment to do a simple gratitude exercise.

1. Sit comfortably and take three deep breaths. Inhale positivity, exhale any tension.
2. Close your eyes and think of five things you are grateful for. These can be small or big—maybe the book in your hands, the food you ate, the sunlight outside or the people in your life.
3. For each thing, say *Thank you, Universe, for this blessing*. Feel the warmth of gratitude in your heart.
4. Smile. Allow yourself to truly feel how blessed you are.

How do you feel? More positive? More aligned? That is the power of gratitude!

The Ultimate Law of Attraction Morning Routine

To maximize the Law of Attraction in your life, you must start your morning with the right energy. Your thoughts in the first hour after waking up set the tone for the rest of your day.

This is why today, I am giving you the ultimate morning routine that will help you stay aligned with your desires, maintain high vibrations and keep attracting what you truly want.

Step 1: Visualization (right after waking up)

The moment you wake up, your mind is in a relaxed state. This is the perfect time for visualization.

- Close your eyes and see yourself already living your dream life.
- If you are manifesting a new job, picture yourself getting the offer letter, sitting at your new desk and feeling proud and accomplished.
- If you are manifesting health, see yourself strong, active and full of energy.
- Add emotion to your visualization. Feel the happiness, excitement and gratitude.

Remember, *The clearer the vision, the stronger the manifestation.*

Step 2: Meditation (minimum fifteen minutes)

Meditation helps to clear your mind, remove doubts and increase your connection with the Universe.

- Find a quiet place, sit comfortably and focus on your breath.
- If your mind wanders, gently bring it back to the present moment.

- You can also do a guided meditation or repeat a mantra like '*I am aligned with my highest good.*'

Tip: Morning meditation reduces stress, increases focus and helps you stay calm throughout the day.

Step 3: Affirmations (choose any one technique)

Affirmations reprogramme your subconscious mind and strengthen your belief system. You can choose any technique from:

- **3-6-9 method:** Write your affirmation three times in the morning, six times in the afternoon and nine times at night.
- **5x55 method:** Write your affirmation fifty-five times a day for five consecutive days.
- **10x3 method:** Write three affirmations ten times each morning until your goals are fulfilled.

The key is to FEEL these affirmations as if they are already true.

Step 4: Physical activity (move your body!)

Your body and mind are connected. To maintain high vibrations, you need to engage in some physical activity.

- This could be a gym workout, yoga, swimming, walking, running or even dancing!

- Moving your body increases endorphins (happy hormones), boosts energy and helps you stay motivated.

Scientific Fact: Exercise releases dopamine and serotonin, which are chemicals that promote positive thinking.

You have reached Day 50, and that is a *massive achievement!* From today onwards, your morning routine will be your foundation. If you follow this daily, the Law of Attraction will work faster and stronger in your life.

> *What you do today becomes your tomorrow; what you do tomorrow becomes your future. So why don't we make the best of today!*
>
> —Dr Amiett Kumar

So, keep going! The Universe is listening. Stay consistent, stay positive, and get ready to attract miracles.

Let's move forward with full energy! You are unstoppable.

Day 51

Healing Relationships—the First Step Begins with You

Let's take a deep breath today.

You've been working on your dreams, on your energy and on your mindset.

But what about those unseen emotional knots?

That sour relationship, that broken friendship, that unspoken misunderstanding?

You may think it's personal or emotional. But in truth—**it affects your vibration.**

Whenever there's pain, resentment or unhealed emotion—whether from family, friends, colleagues or even strangers—it quietly pulls your energy down.

And you already know this:

The Law of Attraction doesn't respond to what you say; it responds to how you feel.

So, today, we take the first step towards healing.

No, we're not calling them.

We're not texting them.

We're not dragging ourselves back into past pain.

We're simply doing what's most powerful in the energetic world of manifestation—we're shifting from within.

Because when energy shifts, relationships follow.

First, let's start our morning in silence. Sit comfortably with your journal.

Write ten good things that happened yesterday. Big or small, it could just be *I had a nice cup of tea* or *my child smiled at me.*

For each one, say:

Thank you, Universe.

Then whisper *thank you* to the person involved.

Why?

When you start the day in gratitude, your heart softens. Your ego relaxes. Your energy expands.

And in that space, we now invite the person we want to heal with.

1. Close your eyes.
2. Bring their image in front of you—not their face during the fight, but the face you once cared for.

Now in your journal, write ten good things about them.

- *She was there for me when I had no one.*
- *He makes my dad smile.*
- *They helped me without asking for anything in return.*

It may feel tough at first. You will face some resistance and mental blocks, but keep writing.

Because the moment you see the *humanity* in them, your energy changes.

And guess what?

Your vibration has now connected with theirs.

This is the real bridge—not words, not calls—but heart-to-heart energetic healing.

The next step—connection with grace

Once you've done this for three days in a row, you will notice a lightness inside. That knot? It will loosen.

At this point, **if you feel called**, reach out.

Send a simple message:

> *Hi, I was thinking of you. Just wanted to say I hope you're doing well.*

That's it. No expectation. No drama. No need to revisit the past.

You're not trying to win. You're trying to heal.

If they don't respond, it's okay. Because you've done your part—and that's the part the Universe honours.

Sometimes, the message is for *them*.

Sometimes, it's for *you*.

Relationships are not broken in a day. They break in silence, misunderstandings and assumptions. But just like cracks can let light in, one step from you can begin the healing.

Even if they don't change, you will.

And that's the real reward: emotional freedom, energetic lightness and inner peace.

So, today, take that first step.

Heal with grace, because when you raise your emotional vibration, the Universe whispers back:

Now you're ready to receive more love in all areas of life.

Day 52

The Secrets of a Millionaire Mind

When you were a kid, what was the one motive that drove you to score the highest marks in class?

I know, it was *chocolates!* Right? Well, I've got some of that chocolate for you today, a prize for all your hard work we have been doing.

Because today's topic is going to be one of the most powerful shifts you'll ever make in your Law of Attraction journey. If you've ever found yourself struggling with money, feeling like you never have enough or wondering why some people seem to attract wealth effortlessly, then today's discussion is for you.

Before we dive in, I want to ask you a simple question:

What is your relationship with money?

- Do you see money as something hard to earn?
- Do you feel guilty about wanting more of it?
- Or do you believe that money flows easily into your life?

Your mindset about money determines how much of it you attract. And today, I want to introduce you to a book that completely transformed my own money mindset:

The Secrets of a Millionaire Mind by T. Harv Eker.

One of the biggest lessons I learnt from this book is that our beliefs about money come from our subconscious programming.

From childhood, we hear things like:

- *Money doesn't grow on trees.*
- *Rich people are greedy.*
- *You have to work extremely hard to make money.*
- *Money is the root of all evil.*

Ever heard any of these?

These beliefs create what Harv Eker calls a 'money blueprint', which is a set of subconscious rules that govern how we handle, attract or repel money.

If you grew up in an environment where money was always a struggle, a stressor or a limited resource, then your mind operates from a scarcity mindset.

But here's the secret:

Millionaires think differently.

Instead of seeing money as something difficult, they see it as a flowing energy: an exchange of value, an opportunity and a tool for growth and impact.

This book teaches practical and powerful ways to change the way you think about money. Here are some of the core lessons that helped me change my life:

1. Rich people think big—poor people think small.

Most people limit their own success by thinking small. They set small financial goals, play it safe, and stay in their comfort zones. But wealthy people think big—they dream bigger, take bigger risks and expect greater rewards.

Ask yourself: *Am I thinking big enough?*

2. Rich people focus on opportunities—poor people focus on obstacles.

A person with a scarcity mindset will always focus on why something won't work: the risks, the failures and the challenges.

But someone with an abundance mindset sees opportunities everywhere. They believe in their ability to create money rather than waiting for someone else to give it to them.

Do you see problems, or do you see possibilities?

3. Rich people are comfortable with being uncomfortable.

If you're afraid to step outside of your comfort zone, you will never grow. The wealthy understand this; they take calculated risks, invest in themselves and push through discomfort.

If you want to attract more money, ask yourself: *Am I willing to do what it takes?*

4. Rich people believe 'I create my life'; poor people believe 'life happens to me.'

This is one of the biggest mindset shifts you need to make. Are you taking full responsibility for your financial reality?

People with a poor mindset blame the economy, the government, their boss or luck. People with a wealthy mindset take control and make things happen.

What excuses are you making? How can you shift from being a victim to a creator?

I used to think that making money was hard. That I had to struggle, work non-stop and sacrifice everything to be wealthy.

But after reading this book, I completely rewired my money mindset.

- I stopped seeing money as something difficult to earn and started seeing it as a tool to create impact and freedom.
- I began practising gratitude for every rupee I earned.
- I let go of limiting beliefs about money and replaced them with empowering ones.
- I started using affirmations and visualization to align myself with abundance.

And guess what? My financial reality changed.

Now, I want you to reflect on your own money mindset.

Take ten minutes to write down the answers to these questions:

- What did you learn about money as a child?
- What are the limiting beliefs you need to let go of?
- How can you start thinking like a millionaire?

If you truly want to attract wealth, you need to think, act and believe like someone who already has it.

Money is energy. Money flows where the right mindset goes.

Are you ready to change yours?

Day 53

Never Say 'No'

Have you ever noticed that when you try really hard **not** to think about something, it somehow keeps popping into your mind? Try this right now:

Do **NOT** think about a blue elephant.

What happened? The image of a blue elephant appeared in your mind, didn't it? That's exactly how the Law of Attraction works!

The Universe doesn't recognize negatives like 'no', 'not' or 'don't'. Instead, it picks up on the core emotion and intent behind your words and thoughts.

Many people unknowingly attract the very things they want to avoid simply by the way they phrase their desires. The Universe works on vibrations; what you focus on expands. So, when you say:

- *I don't want to fail* → the Universe focuses on *failure*.
- *I don't want to be broke* → the Universe focuses on *broke*.

- *I don't want to be sick* → the Universe focuses on *sickness*.

Instead, you need to flip your words into positive affirmations that align with your goals:

- *I want to succeed* → the Universe focuses on *success*.
- *I am attracting more money* → the Universe focuses on *wealth*.
- *I am getting healthier every day* → the Universe focuses on *good health*.

Words are powerful. Every sentence you speak or think sends a direct signal to the Universe. If you constantly focus on things you want to avoid, you will keep attracting them.

Think of it like a GPS:

- If you enter a destination (*I want to be wealthy*), the GPS will guide you there.
- If you enter what you don't want (*I don't want to be broke*), the GPS gets confused and focuses on *broke*.

The Universe does not process the word 'no'; it only sees the focus of your energy.

Here are some common phrases people use that push them further from their goals, and how you can reframe them correctly:

I don't have money.

I am attracting money into my life.

I don't want to fail.

I am achieving success.

I don't want to be alone.
I am attracting meaningful relationships.
I hope I don't mess this up.
I am confident and capable.
I don't want to be stressed.
I am calm, peaceful and in control.
This isn't just spiritual talk; science supports it too.

Neuroscience studies show that negative words and thoughts activate stress responses in the brain, leading to fear, anxiety and self-doubt. On the other hand, positive affirmations activate the reward centres of the brain, boosting confidence and motivation.

Dr Andrew Newberg, a neuroscientist, found that words like 'love' and 'peace' strengthen cognitive function, while negative words like 'no' weaken it.[17] Your brain literally performs better when you use positive words!

Starting today, pay close attention to how you speak about your goals, dreams and desires.

- Whenever you catch yourself using a negative phrase, pause and reframe it into a positive statement.
- Write down three negative thoughts you've had recently and **rephrase** them into positive affirmations.
- Repeat these affirmations for the next twenty-one days and observe how your mindset—and results—begin to shift.

The words you choose today will shape your future reality.

So, the next time you think **I don't want to fail**, stop yourself and say, **I am attracting success!**

Make this small shift and watch how your world transforms.

Day 54

Protect Your Mind

Here is something you should wonder about:

Have you ever noticed how your mood shifts after watching a violent action movie or a tragic news story? That sinking feeling in your chest, the uneasiness that lingers or even the sudden anger or fear—this is how negativity seeps into your subconscious.

Most of us consume negativity daily without realizing it. Whether it's the news, social media, dramatic movies or even toxic conversations, these inputs affect our mindset, emotions and energy levels.

Today, we're going to discuss how to protect your mind while still staying informed and entertained.

Your mind is like a sponge that absorbs whatever you expose it to. Constant exposure to negative media leads to:

1. **Increased stress and anxiety:** Studies show that frequent exposure to negative news increases cortisol levels, leading to stress.

2. **Lower vibrational energy:** According to the Law of Attraction, the emotions you focus on attract similar energies into your life. Constantly absorbing fear, anger or sadness lowers your ability to manifest positivity.

3. **Subconscious programming:** What you see repeatedly becomes your belief system. If all you hear is crime, corruption and suffering, your mind begins to expect negativity in life.

4. **Sleep disturbances:** Watching intense movies or reading distressing news before bed can trigger restlessness and anxiety, making it harder to relax.

Now that we understand why negativity should be minimized, let's discuss how we can consume content mindfully.

We understand that staying informed is important, especially if your job requires it. However, consuming news the wrong way can overwhelm you with unnecessary stress. Here's how to do it wisely:

1. **Set a time limit:** Avoid watching news throughout the day. Check headlines once or twice daily instead of constantly refreshing updates.

2. **Choose neutral sources:** Mainstream news channels often sensationalize negativity. Instead, follow reliable, neutral news sources that focus on facts rather than fear.

3. **Balance negative with positive news:** After reading a heavy news piece, look for uplifting stories—stories of progress, kindness and breakthroughs. Websites

like *The Good News Network* focus on positive journalism.

4. **Avoid news before bed:** The last thing you consume before sleeping affects your subconscious. Switch to uplifting content, books or gratitude exercises before bed instead.

Watching action-packed, horror or tragic films occasionally is okay, but if you're an avid consumer of dark content, it may affect your energy.

If you love such movies, here's how you can neutralize their negative impact:

1. **Watch in moderation:** Instead of binge watching violent movies, mix in light-hearted content (comedies, inspiring documentaries, etc.).
2. **Detach from the emotion:** Remind yourself that it's fiction. If a movie makes you feel uneasy, take deep breaths and ground yourself in reality.
3. **Watch something positive after:** End your screen time with motivational videos, funny content or spiritual teachings to restore balance.
4. **Be mindful of the timing:** Avoid watching horror or action-packed movies right before bed, as they can cause subconscious stress.

If you're looking for ways to stay informed and entertained while keeping your energy high, consider these alternatives:

- **Watch motivational and educational content:** Instead of consuming negativity, try watching TED Talks, inspirational interviews or spiritual discussions.
- **Read personal growth books:** Replace endless scrolling with books that help you grow (*The Secret, Atomic Habits, The Power of Now*).
- **Engage in mindful conversations:** Talk to positive, forward-thinking people instead of indulging in toxic discussions.
- **Follow uplifting social media pages:** Instead of doom-scrolling, follow pages that share good news, self-growth content and motivational insights.
- **Spend time in nature:** Instead of spending hours consuming digital negativity, walk in nature to rejuvenate your energy.

The Law of Attraction works based on the emotions you cultivate daily. If you consume fear, anger and despair, your reality will reflect that. But if you surround yourself with positivity, the Universe will mirror that energy back to you.

Remember, *you are in control of what you allow into your mind*. Choose wisely.

Day 55

My Vision Board Testimony

By now, you already know how powerful a vision board can be. But today, I want to share my own experience—one that proved to me just how powerful the Law of Attraction truly is.

I always wanted to buy a luxury car, and after thorough research and countless discussions, I had narrowed my choices down to BMW and Mercedes. Both brands had their unique appeal, and I went back and forth weighing the pros and cons.

Finally, after careful deliberation, I made my decision: I booked a BMW.

But here's where the real story begins.

A few weeks after booking the BMW, I was casually passing by a Mercedes showroom. Out of sheer curiosity, I walked in and decided to test drive one of their models.

I loved the experience. The drive, the feel, the comfort—it was incredible. But since I had already booked the BMW, I didn't take any further action.

However, there was one small thing I did.

Before leaving the Mercedes showroom, I picked up a brochure and brought it home. Something about the car intrigued me, and I pasted its picture on my vision board.

I didn't think much of it at the time. It was just an image—a simple visual of a car I liked.

Or so I thought.

Over the next three months, a series of unexpected events unfolded:

- ☑ Unforeseen delays and issues—my BMW booking started facing issues—delays in delivery, less clarity of timelines and a series of minor yet frustrating hurdles.
- ☑ A shift in perspective—as I kept looking at my vision board daily, something in me started changing.
- ☑ A final decision—with all the challenges surrounding the BMW booking, I finally decided to cancel the order and go for the same Mercedes I had test-driven earlier.

The best part?

When the Mercedes finally arrived at my doorstep, I went back to my vision board to check the image I had pasted months ago.

It was the exact same model I had just bought!

That moment gave me chills.

This experience wasn't just a coincidence. It was a direct manifestation of what I had unknowingly aligned myself with.

Here's what I learnt from this journey:

- ✔ **Your subconscious mind is powerful**—even though I had initially chosen BMW, my subconscious kept pulling me towards the image on my vision board every single day.

✔ **The Universe pays attention to your visuals**—when you repeatedly see something, your brain accepts it as a reality, and the Universe starts aligning things in your favour.

✔ **Unexpected paths can lead to the right destination**—sometimes, what we initially plan is not what's truly meant for us. The Universe rearranges circumstances to lead us towards what is better aligned with our desires.

✔ **Clarity is key**—the moment I saw the exact same model on my vision board, I realized that I had unintentionally been clearer than I thought about what I truly wanted.

If this story teaches you anything, let it be this:

💡 If you haven't made your vision board yet, make it today.

💡 If you already have one, check if you're actually looking at it daily.

💡 Make sure your vision board represents what you truly want, not what you think you should want.

Your subconscious mind absorbs what it sees regularly, and the Universe will find a way to bring it to you.

And when it does, you'll look back and realize it was always meant to be.

Day 56

The Hottest Question
I'm Always Asked!

Let's play a quick guessing game.

Out of all the questions I get on the Law of Attraction, which one do you think is the most common?

Is it about money? Career? Success?

Nope. None of the above.

The most asked question I get, everywhere I go, is this:

How do I attract a specific person?

Sounds familiar? If you've ever wondered about this, today is your lucky day because we are going to clear all your doubts and give you the exact steps to make this work.

But before we start, I need you to understand one thing:

This is NOT about forcing someone to like you. The Law of Attraction doesn't manipulate people. Instead, it helps you become the best version of yourself—a version so attractive and aligned that the right people naturally gravitate towards you. So, let's dive in.

You might be expecting something complicated, but trust me, this is simple—as long as you follow it with the right mindset.

Scientists say love is a result of chemical reactions; Gen Z says that when you are in love:

Mar mit jayenge, alag nahi honge!

We will do whatever we can, but we will keep LOVING!

So, what is love, and how do you attract it? It is not as complex as solving a law of motion equation, trust me! You just have to follow these simple steps.

Step 1: Love yourself first.

You CANNOT attract love if you don't love yourself. Period.

Think about this—if you don't value yourself, if you constantly feel insecure or unworthy, how will someone else see the best in you?

The Law of Attraction works by mirroring your energy. If you radiate self-love, confidence and happiness, the Universe will send people into your life who reflect those same qualities back to you.

What should you do?

- Work on your self-esteem.

- Take care of yourself physically, emotionally and mentally.
- Spend time doing what you love.
- Stop seeking external validation.
- Affirm every day: *I am lovable. I am enough. I am deserving of great love.*

When you become whole within yourself, you won't feel like you NEED someone—you will simply attract the right one effortlessly.

Step 2: Be clear about what you want.

Most people say, 'I want to attract a specific person.'

But what they really mean is, 'I want someone who makes me feel happy, loved and appreciated.'

You see, what you truly desire is not a person, but the experience of love.

Instead of focusing on one specific person, focus on the qualities you want in your ideal partner.

What should you do?

- Write down the exact qualities you want in a partner (kindness, loyalty, humour, passion, ambition, etc.).
- Visualize yourself with this person. Imagine the emotions, the happiness, the connection.
- Write affirmations: *I am attracting a loving and committed relationship with someone who adores me.*
- Trust that the Universe knows the BEST match for you, and that they WILL arrive at the right time.

Step 3: Become what you want to attract.

Here's the most powerful truth:

You don't attract what you want. You attract what you ARE.

If you want to attract a loving, confident and successful person, ask yourself:

Do I have these qualities myself?

Think about it—would you want to be with someone who is constantly negative, insecure or lost in life?
No, right?
The key is to become the kind of person you want to attract.
What should you do?

- If you want someone kind, be kind to yourself and others.
- If you want someone ambitious, start working on your own dreams.
- If you want someone fun-loving, bring joy into your own life.
- If you want someone trustworthy, be honest in your own actions.

When you embody these qualities, the Universe will naturally align you with the right partner. Manifesting a specific person is not about chasing someone or obsessing over them. It's about:

- *Loving yourself completely.*
- *Being clear about the kind of relationship you want.*
- *Becoming the best version of yourself.*

When you do this, the right person—the one who truly aligns with your soul—will walk into your life at the perfect time.

Until then, focus on YOU. Because the better you feel about yourself, the better the love you will attract. Now, go get to work.

Day 57

The Magic of the Gratitude Stone

Today, we are going to explore a simple yet powerful technique that will help you practise gratitude effortlessly every day—without missing a single day.

But before we begin, grab a small stone or marble. It could be:

- A decorative stone.
- A smooth pebble from the road.
- A small glass marble (*kancha*).

Make sure it is small enough to fit in your pocket or wallet because this little stone is about to become one of the most powerful tools in your Law of Attraction journey.

How, you ask? Well, I'm here to tell you this is how:

Step 1: The power of holding gratitude.

Take your stone and sit in your usual place—the spot where you practise your techniques daily.

Now, hold the stone in your palm. Feel its texture, weight and coolness. This stone is now your **Gratitude Stone**—a reminder of all the wonderful things you have in life.

With the stone in your hand, take a deep breath and say *thank you* out loud.

Now, close your eyes and think about everything in your life that you are grateful for:

- Your health.
- Your family.
- The air you breathe.
- The food on your plate.
- The opportunities you have.
- The little moments of joy in your day.

Let gratitude fill your heart as you hold this stone. This is your moment of positive energy.

Step 2: Carry gratitude with you.

Now, put this stone in your pocket, wallet or purse and carry it with you wherever you go.

Want to know how?

Every time you touch this stone, you must say *thank you* for something in your life.

- If you are at work and your hand brushes against the stone, say *thank you for my job*.
- If you are sitting in a park and feel the stone in your pocket, say *thank you for the fresh air and nature around me*.

- If you are at home and touch the stone, say *thank you for my cozy bed and peaceful home.*

This simple act reprogrammes your brain to automatically find things to be grateful for, making gratitude a natural habit.

Step 3: The nighttime ritual.

Before going to sleep, hold your stone again and think of the **five best things** that happened to you today.
Say:

Thank you for this amazing moment today. I am so grateful for everything in my life.

Feel the joy and appreciation in your heart, then place the stone back in your pocket for the next day.
Why does this work? Intriguing, right?
Because the more you practise gratitude, the more things the Universe will give you to be grateful for.
This practice was inspired by many successful people, including Rhonda Byrne in *The Magic* and spiritual leaders who emphasize the power of tangible reminders to reinforce positive habits.
Science backs this up, too! Studies show that repetitive gratitude practices increase happiness levels and reduce stress.[18] Holding a physical object, like a stone, creates a strong neural connection in the brain, making gratitude a subconscious habit.

A small stone might not seem like much, but when you use it daily, it becomes a powerful force that shifts your mindset, attracts positive energy and helps you stay aligned with abundance.

So, starting today, carry your gratitude stone everywhere and let it remind you to be thankful—because the more gratitude you express, the more miracles will unfold in your life.

Now, take your stone, hold it in your hand, and say:

Thank you, thank you, thank you!

Day 58

The Driving Force Behind
Manifesting Your Desires

HIIIII!

Now, go get your Sherlock hat out! What is a Sherlock hat? You see ,there was this famous detective called Sherlock Holmes; one of the shows based on this character was played by Benedict Cumberbatch, and trust me, his hat picturization is *iconic*!

But why do we need the hat? *Because we are cracking a case today, Sherlock!*

I have received countless testimonials from people who have used the Law of Attraction to achieve their dreams—whether it was financial success, career growth, relationships or personal transformation.

And after analysing so many success stories, I have found two common factors that all of them had:

1. They had unwavering faith in themselves.
2. They believed in Bhagwan, God, the Universe or a supreme power.

Faith and belief: When combined with the right actions, become the ultimate force behind fulfilling desires.

1. Faith in yourself—the unshakeable foundation

'Whether you think you can, or you think you can't—you're right.'

—Henry Ford

The biggest difference between those who achieve their dreams and those who don't is self-belief.

Think about it; if you don't believe in yourself, why would the Universe believe in you?

When you say:

- *I don't think I can do this.*
- *I am not capable.*
- *This is impossible for me.*

. . . then you are sending signals of doubt to the Universe. You are essentially telling the Universe that you are not ready for what you desire.

But when you have faith in yourself, you automatically take actions that lead to success.

- You step out of your comfort zone.
- You take responsibility for your dreams.
- You stay committed even when things get tough.

Success doesn't come from mere thoughts; it comes from self-belief and action.

2. Faith in the Universe—trusting the divine plan

Bhagavad Gita (Chapter 9, Verse 22):

अनन्याश्चिन्तयन्तो मां ये जनाः पर्युपासते |
तेषां नित्याभियुक्तानां योगक्षेमं वहाम्यहम् ||

*To those who are constantly devoted and worship
Me with love, I give the understanding by which they
come to Me.*

Belief in Bhagwan, God or the Universe is what fuels your faith when things seem uncertain.

Manifestation is NOT magic; it is a spiritual and energetic process.

- The Universe has a perfect timeline for you.
- It knows when and how to deliver what you need.
- Your job is to trust the process and keep going.

But this faith is only powerful when combined with action.

3. Faith without action is useless

Here's where many people go wrong: they believe, they visualize and they affirm, but they don't take action.

You cannot just sit and wish for things to happen. The Universe will open doors for you, but YOU have to walk through them.

- If you want to succeed in your business, upskill yourself, work on your network and work consistently.
- If you want a healthy life, eat healthy, think positive and keep working out as much as possible.
- If you want love, work on self-love and become the person you want to attract.

4.   The power of consistency

The most successful manifesters I have met had one thing in common—they were consistent.

- They didn't visualize once and forget about it.
- They didn't write affirmations for a week and quit.
- They didn't meditate for a few days and lose hope.

Instead,

- They practised visualization every morning.
- They wrote affirmations daily.
- They practised gratitude without fail.
- They took consistent actions towards their goals.

If you truly want to fulfil your desires, you must:

1. **Believe in yourself.** Without this, nothing moves.
2. **Trust the Universe.** Let it handle the *how*.
3. **Take action.** Nothing happens without action.
4. **Stay consistent.** Small steps daily lead to massive success.

Faith + action = manifestation success!

Now, take a moment to reflect:

> *Are you applying both faith and action in your journey?* If not, start today!

Your dreams are waiting; go claim them!

Day 59

The Power of Thought Vibrations

Have you ever had a moment where you are doing something and suddenly feel like you have done this exact thing before, in the same position and environment?

It's not quite déjà vu this time; it's real.

Think about it; has this ever happened to you?

Maybe you were thinking about an old friend, and suddenly, they called you out of nowhere. Maybe you were considering buying a new car, and suddenly, you started seeing that exact model everywhere.

This is not a coincidence. This is the power of thought vibrations at work.

Every thought you have carries energy.

This energy sends signals to the Universe, and those signals bring more of the same kind of energy back to you.

- The stronger your thoughts, the stronger the vibrations you send out.
- The more frequently you think about something, the more you notice it in your reality.

Let's say you start thinking about getting new plants for your home.

- Suddenly, on your way to work, you notice every nursery and plant shop that you have never paid attention to before.
- You see the greenery around you more vividly.
- You even start noticing different kinds of flowers and their unique fragrances.

Why does this happen?

Because the moment you shift your focus to something, your mind aligns itself to receive more of it.

This phenomenon is linked to something called the reticular activating system (RAS) in neuroscience. Remember we discussed it earlier?

Your RAS is a part of your brain that acts like a filter.

- It decides what information is important and what is irrelevant.
- It magnifies the things that you focus on the most.

That's why when you start thinking about something—whether it's a goal, a desire or even a worry—your RAS makes sure you notice more of it around you.

- If you think about positivity, you will attract positive experiences.
- If you think about struggles, you will find more struggles appearing in your life.

The Law of Attraction works through thought vibrations. The energy you put out is the energy you attract.

It all comes down to what you choose to focus on.

Your thoughts shape your reality.

The more you focus on something, the more the Universe brings it into your life.

1. Be intentional with your thoughts.
2. Think in the direction of what you want, not what you don't want.
3. Train your mind to align with your desires.

Your mind is your most powerful tool—use it wisely!

Day 60

Manifesting Your Dream House

Today is a special day because we are focusing on manifesting your dream home. If you've ever wondered how to bring your ideal house into reality, this is the chapter that will set you on the right path.

But first, let me share my own story of how I manifested my dream home.

When I decided I wanted to buy a house, I had no money to make that decision.

Logically, it didn't seem possible at the time. But I had two things that mattered more than anything:

- My belief in the Law of Attraction
- My trust in the Universe

I knew that if I aligned my energy with the reality of homeownership, the Universe would open the right doors for me.

Basically, I acted as if I was already in the process of buying a house.

I put the thought out into the Universe, and I programmed my subconscious to believe that we were actually doing this.

And guess how it happened! One day I had a friend over at my house for tea, and we were chatting when the subject of buying a house popped up in our conversation.

He showed me a brochure he had for a house in a well-to-do society and we discussed the topic wholeheartedly.

After my friend went home, I realized he had left the brochure on the table we were chatting at. I didn't pay it much mind at that time.

A little while later, when we were browsing for properties, a real estate dealer got in contact with us and asked for us to visit one of the properties he felt would be the right fit for us.

I went to the place he mentioned, and we toured the house that my wife, Aadhyaa, and I really loved. When we returned to our home at that time, I was sorting through some magazines in the cupboard when I saw the brochure that my friend had left.

Want to know why that brochure is so important? It was the brochure for the exact same society we had just visited and were debating on buying into!

A few days later, our decision was made, and we bought our own house in the same society.

Many people think that manifestation means just sitting and visualizing something without taking action. But that's not how it works.

The moment you start taking real, physical action, you show the Universe that you are serious about your dream.

- By physically visiting houses, I sent a clear signal that I was ready for this reality.
- This triggered opportunities, and step by step, I made my dream a reality.

If you want to manifest your own home, start with these simple but powerful steps:

1. **Start exploring homes in your desired location**

Even if you think buying a house isn't possible right now, go visit the places you want to live in.

- Walk through the neighbourhood.
- Visit model homes or open houses.
- Take a tour of apartments or villas that align with your dream.

2. **Absorb the experience as if it's already yours**

While you are in these houses, act as if they are already yours.

1. Imagine where your furniture would go.
2. Feel yourself walking through the rooms every morning.
3. Touch the walls and say, 'This is my home.'

3. **Repeat these thoughts daily:**

- This home is already mine; I am aligning with it.

- I am on my way to my dream home.

The more you believe it, the faster you align with the opportunities to make it happen.

I didn't wait for my house to magically appear; I started acting like it was already mine.

And guess what? Step by step, the right opportunities showed up, and I was able to buy my dream home.

Now, it's your turn.

- Start looking at homes.
- Visit neighbourhoods.
- Put the thought out into the Universe.

And most importantly—take action with a positive mindset.

Your dream house is already waiting for you—now it's time for you to claim it.

Day 61

Manifesting for Your Loved Ones

There is a very famous question that I have been asked in my YouTube videos. It is also a very intriguing question, which I got asked for the first time.

'Can we manifest for our loved ones?'

Today, we are diving into something new and powerful—using the Law of Attraction for other people but only for our family and our loved ones.

But first, let's start our day with a gratitude exercise.

Before we get into today's lesson, get up and go to the nearest family member or friend you can find.

- Give them a warm hug without any reason, just because you are grateful for them.
- If they ask why, just smile and say, 'Because I appreciate you.'

Done?

Go sit in the usual spot where you sit and focus on yourself and do your daily exercise. Now, tell me, did they smile? Did you smile?

That small act of kindness just raised your energy vibrations. Feeling good yet? That's the power of positive emotions, and today, we are using this power for our loved ones.

Many people ask, 'Can I manifest something for someone else?'

The answer is YES! The Law of Attraction isn't limited to your own goals alone; you can use it to send positive energy towards the people you love.

So how do we get it done?

1. When you visualize and affirm something for someone else, your energy and vibrations rise.
2. The moment that person comes in contact with you, this energy is transferred to them.
3. This increases their belief, positivity and motivation, even if they don't know you're doing it!

Sounds magical, right? But this is how energy works.

Let's break this down into a simple process that you can follow starting today.

1. Write affirmations for them

Pick someone in your family or a close friend. Think about something they deeply desire.

Now, write an affirmation on their behalf as if it has already happened.

For example:

- If your brother wants a job:
  Thank you, Universe! My brother has just received his dream job, and he is so happy and successful in his career.

- If your mother wants good health:
  Thank you, Universe! My mother is healthy, energetic and living a joyful life.

- If your friend wants to pass an exam:
  Thank you, Universe! My friend has passed with amazing grades, and they are so proud of themselves.

The key is to put emotions into it; feel the happiness as if it has already happened.

2. Visualize their success

Once you have written the affirmation, close your eyes and visualize them achieving it.

1. Imagine their reaction—see them smiling, celebrating, feeling joyful.
2. Feel their happiness as if it's your own.
3. Picture them telling you the good news and hugging you in excitement.

This step is crucial because the more emotions you pour into it, the more powerful it becomes.

3. Keep your energy high around them

Here's the most interesting part—you don't even need to tell them you are doing this!

Just do one simple thing:

When you see them, smile and say, 'It will happen; you got this.'

Your belief will transfer energy to them, making them feel more confident about their goal.

Everything in the Universe is energy. Thoughts, words and emotions carry vibrations.

This is one of the most powerful things you can do. Imagine how much positive energy you can create when you start using the Law of Attraction for your loved ones.

So, let's start today:

1. Pick someone in your family.
2. Write an affirmation for them.
3. Visualize their success.
4. When you see them, smile and say, 'It will happen.'

They don't need to know you are doing this for them, but they will feel it.

The Universe listens to love.

Day 62

Bonus Tips for Writing Affirmations

Let's start today with a small reflection.

Take a moment and recall the affirmations you have been writing since we started this journey.
Now, ask yourself these questions:

- How do you feel when you write your affirmations?
- Do you feel more confident and positive about your desires?
- Have you noticed any small or big changes in your mindset since you started this practice?

Take a moment to write down your thoughts below.

My experience with writing affirmations so far:

____

____

Now that you've had a moment to reflect, let's move on to some powerful bonus tips that I have personally discovered through years of practice. These small changes have made a big impact on my affirmation practice, and I want to share them with you.

Now, since we have been working together so hard for this long, here are some bonus tips for writing affirmations.

1. Use a sheet of yellow paper

Yellow represents optimism, mental clarity and energy. It is believed to enhance focus and make your affirmations more effective. Writing on a yellow sheet helps imprint your affirmations into your subconscious mind more easily.

If you don't have yellow sheets right now, don't worry! You can always start this practice when you get them.

2. Use a red or green pen

Red symbolizes power, passion and strong energy. It enhances the emotional intensity behind your affirmations, making them more effective.

Green represents growth, prosperity, and abundance. If you're writing money-related affirmations, a green pen can amplify your intentions.

These colours subconsciously align your mind with the energy you are manifesting.

3. Avoid using a black pen

Black is associated with neutrality, seriousness and sometimes even restrictions. From my experience, black ink lacks the vibrancy needed to create an energetic connection with your affirmations.

Instead, use colours that evoke strong emotions and positive energy.

A gentle reminder: These are add-ons, not rules. If you don't have a yellow sheet or a coloured pen right now, don't stress! Continue writing your affirmations as you have been doing.

When your current diary is full, you can start applying these suggestions. The most important thing is consistency and emotions, not the medium.

Your task for today

- Review your current affirmations.
- Try using a yellow sheet with a red or green pen for the next few days.
- Observe if you feel any difference in energy or effectiveness.

These small changes can elevate your manifestation practice. Try them out and see what works best for you!

Day 63

The Power of Restarting—a Lesson from Jap Mala

Today, we are going to learn a valuable lesson from an age-old spiritual practice: chanting with a jap mala.

If you've ever used a jap mala (a string of 108 beads) during meditation or chanting, you might already know the answer to this:

What do you do when you lose count in the middle of your chant?

You restart! No questions, no frustration; just a simple reset with the same devotion and energy.

This is exactly the mindset we need to cultivate in our Law of Attraction practice.

When practising Law of Attraction techniques—whether it's affirmations, visualizations, 10x3, the 3-6-9 method or the water technique—consistency is the key to success.

But what happens if you miss a day? Or if you break the rhythm?

- You don't panic.
- You don't doubt yourself.
- You restart with the same belief and enthusiasm.

Imagine you are doing the 3-6-9 method for forty-five days, and on Day 44, you forget to complete your last set of affirmations. What should you do?

You restart from Day 1 with full energy.

At first, restarting might feel frustrating. You might think, 'Why do I have to start over when I was so close?' But here's the shift in perspective you need:

- Every restart reinforces your intention. The more you repeat, the stronger the belief becomes.
- The Universe always listens. It sees your commitment and rewards you accordingly.
- Repetition deepens your subconscious alignment. Just like muscle memory, your thoughts and desires become stronger with practice.

If you miss a day and restart with frustration, it defeats the purpose.

Wrong approach:

- *Oh no, I messed up! Now I have to start all over again.*

Right approach:

- *Great! I get another chance to reinforce my goal and align even better.*

See the difference? The way you look at it changes everything.

1. If you have been practising a Law of Attraction technique and missed a day or broke the flow, restart it today with a fresh mindset.
2. Use this opportunity to refine your affirmations and visualization process.
3. Think of it as a jap mala practice—every bead brings you closer to your goal.

The journey is as important as the destination. Embrace every restart with joy, and you'll see the magic unfold!

Day 64

Digital vs Real Books—Which One Wins?

Let's start today with an interesting debate-worthy question:

Digital vs Real Books—Which is Better?

Some of you might say that digital books are convenient, accessible anywhere and easy to carry. Others might argue that **real books** give a personal, immersive experience—allowing you to highlight, underline and physically connect with the knowledge inside.

So, which one is actually better?

The truth is, both have their own advantages, but when it comes to practising the Law of Attraction, there is one crucial rule:

You MUST physically write your affirmations.

Now, why is this so important? Let's understand this using an analogy you'll never forget.

Let's take an example from a game almost everyone has played at some point:

Temple Run / Subway Surfers

Imagine this:

You're playing Temple Run on your phone, making your character run endlessly, dodging obstacles and collecting coins.

But here's the question:

Does your character running in the game make YOU physically fit?

Of course not!

Just because your game avatar is running, it doesn't mean you are actually exercising or improving your fitness in real life.

Now, apply this logic to affirmations.

- Typing affirmations on your phone or laptop is like Temple Run—it's just a passive action that doesn't truly engage your mind and body.
- Writing affirmations by hand, on paper, is like actual running—it engages your thoughts, focus, energy and intention on a much deeper level.

This is why physically writing affirmations is far more powerful than just typing them into your mobile notes app.

Writing by hand has been scientifically proven to have significant advantages over typing:

1. **Stronger brain connection:** Studies show that writing things down activates more areas of the brain compared to typing. This helps in memory retention and deepens your subconscious alignment with what you are writing.
2. **Stronger emotional connection:** When you physically write something, it feels more real and personal, creating a deeper emotional bond with your goals.
3. **Higher manifestation energy:** The effort, movement and focus required for handwriting create a stronger vibrational frequency that aligns with the Universe.
4. **Increased commitment:** Writing affirmations by hand makes you more invested in them. When you take the time to write them out daily, it builds a habit of discipline and focus.

Simply put, writing affirmations is an active process that deeply embeds your desires into your subconscious mind, making them more likely to manifest in reality.

Here is what you must do:

1. If you've been typing affirmations on your phone, start writing them by hand starting today.
2. Use a dedicated journal or a yellow sheet with red/ green ink, as we discussed earlier.
3. Take five to ten minutes daily to write your affirmations, feeling each word as you write. Imagine your desires coming true with every stroke of the pen.

4. Read your written affirmations aloud after writing them to further strengthen their impact.
5. Carry your affirmation journal with you and revisit your affirmations whenever you feel the need to realign your focus.

Here is something for you to process:

1. Would you rather watch a workout video or actually exercise?
2. Would you rather play a running game or actually go for a run?

Similarly, would you rather type your affirmations passively or write them with full energy and intention?

When you physically write something down, you declare it to the Universe with more conviction than a simple typed note.

The Law of Attraction responds to energy, and writing carries a much higher energy frequency than typing.

This is why you should promise yourself that, from today onwards, you will write your affirmations with purpose, with belief and with the energy of already having achieved them.

The Universe is listening. Pick up your pen and start writing!

Day 65

Healing Your Skin and Health with the Water Technique

Let's take a moment to reflect: have you ever noticed how placebo treatments sometimes heal people just because they believe they are taking real medicine?

This is because our mind, thoughts and beliefs have a powerful impact on our body—and today, we are going to tap into that power to heal ourselves.

Many ancient cultures, spiritual traditions and even modern research suggest that water carries energy and has the ability to absorb and transmit information. Just like we discussed on Day 17.

So today, we are going to revisit and apply the **water technique** specifically for healing skin diseases and improving overall health.

Scientific evidence:

1. **Quantum biology and mind-body connection:** Research in epigenetics by Dr Bruce Lipton suggests

that our thoughts and beliefs can influence our body's ability to heal itself by activating or deactivating certain genetic expressions.[19]

2. **Water and cells in our body:** The human body is 70 per cent water, which means that, just like in Emoto's experiments, our internal water structure is influenced by our emotions and thoughts. If we consistently send positive energy to the water inside us, it can promote cell regeneration, better hydration and healing at a deeper level.

Now, let's apply this knowledge practically.

The **water technique** works by infusing healing vibrations, positivity and belief into water before drinking it.

Now, here's how you can do it.

Step 1: Find a peaceful spot. Sit in a calm place where you won't be disturbed.

Step 2: Take a glass of water. Hold it in both hands. It can be regular water, warm water or herb-infused water.

Step 3: Speak or think positive affirmations.

- Say any affirmation directly into the water.
- Examples:

  o *This water is healing every cell in my body.*
  o *My skin is glowing, healthy and free from any disease.*

Step 4: Drink slowly and mindfully.

- As you drink, imagine the water healing your cells.
- Feel gratitude as the water nourishes you.

Step 5: Repeat twice a day for thirty days.

- Practise this morning and night, as many times as you can for at least one month to see results.

Real-life cases of healing through intention and water

Case Study 1: Lourdes miracles

- The Lourdes water in France is believed to have miraculous healing powers and has been linked to over 7000 unexplained healings.
- People believe it absorbs prayers and intentions from those who visit, much like the water technique works when we infuse positive energy into it.

Case Study 2: Tibetan healing rituals

- Tibetan monks have used mantra-infused water for centuries, where they chant healing words over water before drinking it.
- Many practitioners believe this water boosts immunity, calms the mind and promotes inner healing.

Case Study 3: Modern scientific validation

- Studies have found that patients who believed in their treatment recovered faster, even if they were unknowingly taking a placebo.[20]
- This means that belief and intention alone can amplify the effectiveness of healing.

If you want the fastest results, make sure to:

- Be consistent—drink positively charged water daily.
- Feel gratitude—the more grateful you feel, the stronger the vibrations.
- Use glass containers—avoid plastic bottles, as glass retains energy better.
- Pair with healthy habits—eat well, exercise and sleep properly for holistic healing.

Your cells, thoughts and beliefs are all interconnected. If you constantly think negatively about your health, your body will respond with more illness and discomfort.

But when you start feeding your body with positive energy, gratitude and healing intentions, it will begin to repair itself faster than you ever imagined. Start the water healing technique today.

Drink with intention, believe in the process, and trust that your body is healing with every sip.

Day 66

Can Someone Use the Law of Attraction to Harm You?

Let's address a common **myth**:

Can someone who dislikes me use the Law of Attraction against me? Or can someone harm me using tona-totka, kaala jaadu *or negative manifestation?*

The answer is NO. Absolutely not.

The Law of Attraction is a pure, universal force that only works for positivity. It is not magic; it operates based on what we radiate and how we align ourselves with the Universe.

1. The Law of Attraction responds to the thinker

- What you focus on expands.
- If someone is thinking negatively about you, they are aligning themselves with negativity, not you.

2. Vibrations must align for manifestation

• The Law of Attraction works through alignment. If
   you maintain high vibrations (positivity, confidence,
   peace), someone else's negativity cannot affect you.
• Just like a radio station, if you're tuned to 101.6 FM,
   you won't hear 89.2 FM.

3. Negativity comes back to them

• What we send out, we receive.
• If someone wishes harm for you, they are attracting
   harm for themselves.
• Haven't we discussed this? What goes around, comes
   around.

If you are calm and focused, and someone comes to you
shouting angrily, will it disturb you?

• Only if you let it.
• If you remain positive, their anger cannot impact you.

If you are filled with love and confidence, will someone's
insult break you?

• No. Their words only have power if you give them
   power.

The same applies to the Law of Attraction.
   As long as you stay in a positive vibration, negativity
bounces off you like raindrops on an umbrella.

Some people fear that someone can manifest something bad in their life.

But let's debunk this using Law of Attraction principles:

1. Black magic works on fear, not power.

•   It can only affect you if you believe in it and align your energy with fear.
•   If you ignore it, it has zero impact.

2. Protect yourself with high vibrations.

•   Being grateful, happy and positive forms an energetic shield.

3. What you focus on expands.

•   If you keep thinking someone is trying to harm you, you start attracting fear.
•   Instead, focus on positivity and nothing can touch you.

Don't think bad of others, even if they are your enemy!
Why?

Because if you do, you attract that negativity back into your own life.

If someone constantly wishes bad things for others, what happens?

Their life fills with anger, jealousy and frustration. Meanwhile, the person they wished bad for moves forward.

That's the real power of the Law of Attraction.

- **Stay positive:** focus on what you want, not on what others say.
- **Practise gratitude:** keeps your vibration high.
- **Meditate and affirm:** strengthens your energy.
- **Avoid gossip and negativity:** these lower your vibrations.
- **Bless everyone:** even if someone dislikes you, send them peace—it keeps you safe.

Nobody controls your destiny except you.

The Universe responds to your energy, thoughts, and focus.

So instead of worrying about negative people, bad intentions, or 'tona-totka', simply focus on raising your own vibrations.

The higher your energy, the less anything negative can touch you.

So, what are you going to focus on today?

Day 67

What Language Should You Use for Affirmations?

Ah, here we go again—another **classic** Law of Attraction doubt.

'Sir, which language should I write my affirmations in? English, Hindi, French or . . . Sanskrit?'

'Kya Universe ko sirf angrezi samajh aati hai?'

(Does the Universe understand only English?)

I love this question because it cracks me up every time!

Let's settle this once and for all.

Let's break this down logically.

Think about it—if the Universe **only** understood one language, wouldn't that mean that only people who speak that language would manifest their dreams?

That would mean:

- An English speaker could easily manifest a Ferrari. A Hindi speaker would only get a Maruti.
- A French speaker would be sipping champagne in Paris. Meanwhile, a Bhojpuri speaker would just get lassi in Varanasi.

Sounds ridiculous, right? **Exactly!**

The Universe is limitless—it doesn't care about language. What it actually understands is energy, emotions and vibrations.

Imagine this:

Let's say a person from China, a person from Spain and a person from India all want to manifest a dream job.

◇ The Chinese person says: 谢谢宇宙 (Thank you, Universe!)
◇ The Spanish person says: *Gracias, Universo!*
◇ The Indian person says: *Dhanyawad, Brahmand!*

Now, do you really think the Universe will respond to only one of them?

Is it sitting somewhere with a giant Google Translate button?

NO! The Universe responds to emotions, not words.

Simple: Whatever language you are most comfortable in.

- If Hindi feels natural, write in Hindi.
- If English feels powerful, write in English.
- If your heart connects with Urdu, Bengali, Tamil, Marathi or even Pig Latin, go for it!

It's not about words; it's about the energy you put behind them.

Here's another fun way to think about it.

If you say 'turn on the lights' to your voice assistant, it will switch them on, right?

But what happens if you angrily scream it?

Will Alexa say:

'Sir, aap gussa kyun ho rahe ho? Mai toh bas bulb jalane ki koshish kar rahi thi!'

(Sir, why are you angry? I was just trying to turn on the lightbulb.)

Of course not! It only understands the words, not your emotions.

But the Universe is the exact opposite—it ignores the words and responds only to emotions!

That's why:

- Saying 'I am abundant' with excitement = attracting abundance.
- Saying 'I am abundant' with doubt = attracting struggle.

The words are just a tool to focus your energy.

The real secret is:

1. Feel the affirmation in your heart
2. Visualize it deeply
3. Speak it as if it has already happened

That's how you make the Universe listen.

So, whether you say 'I am successful' or 'Mai safal hoon' or 'Je suis réussi', what matters is that you believe it with your whole heart.

So, don't stress about whether your affirmations are in English, Hindi, Tamil or Hinglish ('*Mujhe ek badiya wali life chahiye, Universe bhaiya, de do na!*').

The Universe isn't marking your affirmations like a schoolteacher.

What matters is:

• Feeling the emotions.
• Believing in the process.
• Stay consistent.

And trust me, no language barrier can stop your dreams from coming true!

Day 68

Your Thoughts Define Your Limits!

Let's start today with an interesting thought experiment.

Imagine you are about to run a race. Just before the race begins, someone tells you,

'The fastest time anyone has ever run this track is in ten minutes. No one has ever done it faster.'

Now, imagine another scenario where you are just told,

'Run as fast as you can and break your limits!'

Which situation do you think will push you to go faster?

This is exactly what we are discussing today—how our mindset defines our limits and how those limits can either propel us forward or hold us back.

Let me share a powerful real-life corporate experiment that proves this concept.

A well-known company hired twenty students from a top business school for their sales department.

They divided them into two groups of ten and gave them the same sales training, the same resources and the same goals.

The only difference?

- Group A was told that the highest sales ever achieved by one person were Rs 100 crore.
- Group B was told nothing about past records or sales limits.

What happened after one month?

☑ Group A: Since they knew the highest sale ever recorded was Rs 100 crore, they unconsciously limited their efforts to match that benchmark. Their top performers reached close to Rs 100 crore but did not exceed it.

☑ Group: Without any mental limits, this group had no fixed benchmark to stop at. Their best performers reached sales of Rs 200 crore, doubling what Group A achieved.

This experiment proves a simple but life-changing truth:

As far as our thoughts can reach, we can reach there too.

In simple terms:

☑ If you believe you can only achieve Rs 10 lakh, you will never aim for Rs 1 crore.

☑ If you believe you can only run 5 km, you will never attempt 10 km.

☑ If you believe success is hard, it will always remain difficult.

Your mind creates the limits that define how far you go.

The moment you remove these limitations, your real potential begins to unfold.

Want another scientifically proven case?

For decades, athletes believed that no human could run a mile in under four minutes. Doctors and scientists even claimed it was physically impossible.

Then came Roger Bannister in 1954. He broke the barrier and ran a mile in three minutes and fifty-nine seconds.

The shocking part?

Within the next two years, over thirty more athletes ran a mile in under four minutes!

What changed? Not human biology.

Only belief. Once the mental barrier was broken, runners around the world realized, 'If Bannister did it, why can't we?'

Here's what you need to do:

1. Stop limiting yourself with past records.

- Don't ask *How much can I earn based on my qualifications?*
- Instead, ask *How can I earn 10x more?*

2. Surround yourself with limitless thinkers.

- Talk to people who dream big, think big and act big.
- If you always hear *This is not possible*, your brain will believe it.

- If you hear *Anything is possible*, your brain will start looking for ways to make it happen.

3. Set goals beyond your imagination.

- If you think Rs 10 lakh is your max, set a goal for Rs 1 crore.
- If you think you can only lose 5 kg, set a goal for 15 kg.

4. Use the Law of Attraction to expand your vision.

- Write affirmations such as
  I am achieving more than I ever imagined.
- Visualize yourself breaking limits.
- Believe that you deserve bigger and better things.

You are as powerful as you allow yourself to be.
You are only as successful as you believe you can be.
So, today, make a decision.

- Think beyond limits.
- Believe beyond boundaries.
- Achieve beyond expectations.

Because the only thing standing between you and your dreams . . . is the size of your thinking.

Day 69

The Power of the Gratitude Jar

Let's begin with a light exercise

Before we dive into today's special discussion, let's get our body and mind aligned. Stand up, stretch your arms, roll your shoulders back and take a few deep breaths.

Now, do ten slow squats or just jog in place for thirty seconds. Feel the energy flow in your body.

Done? Good! Now, take a seat in your **usual spot**—the one where you sit every day to practise your techniques, focus and relax.

Close your eyes for a moment. Take a deep breath in, hold it for four seconds and slowly breathe out. Repeat this a few times until you feel calm and centred.

Now that you're ready, let's talk about something truly magical—the **Gratitude Jar**.

This simple yet powerful technique is something I personally practise, and I can tell you with full conviction that the energy it generates is beyond comparison.

So how do we do it?

1. Every time something good happens to you, take a small slip of paper.
    Write this sentence: *Thank you Universe for* ________.
    (Fill in the blank with what you are grateful for.)

2. Take a glass jar (or a box) and place the slip inside.
3. Keep adding slips whenever you feel grateful about something.

Over time, this jar will fill up with gratitude—a tangible reminder of all the positivity in your life.

At the end of the month or the year, sit down with your jar, open it and read each gratitude slip one by one.

You will realize something powerful:

• How many amazing things have happened in your life.
• How much progress you have made.
• How blessed you actually are.

This one simple act of reflecting on gratitude will instantly uplift your energy and emotions to an entirely different level.

Trust me, the positive vibrations you will experience are unparalleled.

When I first started this practice, my jar was almost empty for the first few weeks.

It's not because I didn't have things to be grateful for. It was because I wasn't aware of how many things I should be appreciating in my life.

This happens to everyone in the beginning. We overlook the small joys and only recognize the bigger milestones.

But with time, as you train your mind to focus on gratitude, you will start noticing the smallest blessings.

Soon, your jar will be filled with:

* Moments of happiness
* Achievements, big or small
* Kind words from people
* Unexpected good news
* Simple joys like a great meal, good health or peaceful sleep

You have two choices:

1. Make it a year-long practice—start now and fill your jar until 31 December. Then, at the end of the year, celebrate everything you were grateful for.
2. Make it a monthly practice—start afresh every month and review your gratitude slips at the end of each month. This gives you quick boosts of positivity every thirty days!

It's completely up to you. The key is consistency.

Gratitude isn't just a spiritual concept; it's backed by science.

Studies show[21] that people who actively practise gratitude experience:

* Less stress and anxiety
* Improved sleep quality

- Stronger immune system
- Increased happiness and life satisfaction

Why? Because when you focus on what's good in your life, your brain releases dopamine and serotonin, the two neurotransmitters responsible for making you feel happy.

In simple terms:

The more you express gratitude, the happier and healthier you become.

You may have heard this before:

The more grateful you are, the more you will receive.

This is one of the core principles of the Law of Attraction.

By practising gratitude every day, you are telling the Universe:

I appreciate what I have, and I am ready for more.

The Universe listens, and sends even more reasons for you to be grateful!

So, grab a jar, start your gratitude journey today, and watch how your life transforms.

Day 70

What You Sow, So Shall You Reap

Let's begin with a quick test!
Imagine this scenario:

You're walking home after a long day, feeling relaxed
and content. Suddenly, you see a stranger sitting on
a bench, looking extremely sad. His shoulders are
slumped, and his eyes seem distant, lost in thought.

Now, you have two choices:

A. Ignore him and think to yourself:
    *He looks upset, but it's none of my business. I'm glad
    my day was good. I should just keep walking and not
    get involved.*

B. Approach him and say something kind:
    *Hey, I don't know what's bothering you, but I just
    wanted to let you know that things will get better.*

You're stronger than you think. If you need someone to talk to, I'm here to listen.

Which one would you choose?

If your answer is Option B, congratulations! You've already understood the essence of today's lesson. But keep reading, because the real magic lies ahead!

Most people instinctively choose Option A—not because they are bad people, but because it's easier.

- They think: *Why should I interfere in someone else's life?*
- They assume: *I have my own problems; why should I care about his?*
- Or they justify: *Someone else will help him.*

This is a selfish mindset—and not in a way that benefits you. Because when you train yourself to ignore people's pain, you unknowingly programme the Universe to ignore you when you are in need.

If you consistently turn away from those who need help, the day you need help, people will turn away from you.

This is the law of cause and effect.

What you give, you receive. What you sow, you reap.

Now, let's talk about Option 2.

Let's say you chose to help that stranger.

- Your kind words lift his spirits.
- He starts believing that *maybe things will be okay.*

- He regains strength to face his problems.

A few days later, when he sees someone else struggling, he remembers your kindness and pays it forward.

- This is how positivity compounds.
- This is how kindness spreads.
- This is how you create a world where help is abundant.

Now, imagine this:

- You help one person today.
- Tomorrow, that one person helps someone else.
- The next day, two more people help two more people.

Very soon, without even realizing it, you have created an entire web of people who are ready to help each other.

And when the day comes that you need a helping hand, you won't find just one.

You will find a thousand hands reaching out to support you!

The Law of Attraction works on energy and vibrations.

When you put good energy into the Universe, it multiplies and comes back to you in ways you never expected.

- If you give love, you receive love.
- If you give kindness, you receive kindness.
- If you offer help, the Universe ensures that you get help when you need it most.

On the other hand:

- If you ignore people's pain, the Universe might place you in a situation where you feel ignored.
- If you hold back kindness, the Universe might hold back kindness from you.

This is not punishment—it is balance.

The Universe is always watching and listening. It mirrors your actions and gives you back exactly what you put in.

Thought for the Day

If you help people in need, then on the day you need one hand, a thousand will come to help you instead.

This is not just a saying; this is a spiritual law that has been proven time and again.

If you truly want to attract abundance, happiness and success, start by being the source of those things for others.

Even small acts of kindness can change the world around you.

- Smile at a stranger.
- Say a kind word to someone having a bad day.
- Offer guidance when someone asks for help.

Because in the end, what you sow, so shall you reap.

Day 71

The Real Meaning of the Law of Attraction—Attract + Action

Here's a fact I am pretty sure most of you missed. Because let's be honest, even I did not get it at first.

Attraction is made up of two words: **Attract + Action.**

You may have heard people say, 'I believe in the Law of Karma,' which means they believe in taking action and getting things done.

But then comes the question:

What is the difference between the Law of Attraction and the Law of Karma?

If both emphasize action, why do we need the Law of Attraction at all?

Today, we will break this down with clarity, logic and spiritual wisdom.

The Law of Karma is simple—it states that whatever action you take, you will get a reaction.

कर्मण्येवाधिकारस्ते मा फलेषु कदाचन ।
मा कर्मफलहेतुर्भूर्मा ते सङ्गोऽस्त्वकर्मणि ॥

This verse from the Bhagavad Gita (Chapter 2, Verse 47) is one of the most powerful explanations of karma. It states:

'You have the right to perform your prescribed duty, but you are not entitled to the fruits of your actions.'

This means your job is to act, but the results are in the hands of a higher power.

Now, this brings up an important question:

If I work hard but have no control over the results, how do I ensure that my actions are always leading to success?

This is where the Law of Attraction comes in.

While karma (action) is necessary, attraction (energy, vibration and belief) plays an equally important role.

Think about this:

- If you are confused about your goal, how can your actions be effective?
- If you feel doubtful about success, won't your actions reflect that doubt?
- If you are working hard but feeling miserable, will that work be as productive as it could be?

This is the problem that many people face. They take action, but because they are not in the right mindset, their actions do not lead to success.

This is why the Law of Attraction teaches us to work on our thoughts, emotions, and clarity first!

- When you are positive, your actions are powerful.
- When you are confident, your results are precise.
- When you are clear, you move in the right direction.

Thus, before we act, we must first attract.

When you practise affirmations, visualizations, meditation and gratitude, what are you doing?

You are creating a powerful, focused and positive mindset.

Let's compare two individuals:

Person A: Takes action without working on his mindset.

Person B: Uses the Law of Attraction to first align his thoughts and emotions before taking action.

Who do you think will succeed faster?

Person A is confused, stressed and doubtful. His actions are random, his decisions are unclear and his results are inconsistent.

Person B is confident, motivated and focused. His actions are precise, his decisions are aligned and his results are fast and successful.

In the Mahabharata, Lord Krishna explains:

'Your mind is the bow, your actions are the arrows, and your success is the target. If your bow (mind) is weak, no matter how strong your arrows (actions) are, they will never hit the target (success).'

This is why working on our thoughts, emotions and vibrations first is essential.

If we take action without aligning ourselves mentally, we might still succeed, but it will be slow, painful and inefficient.

However, if we first train our mind to be focused, positive and determined, then every action we take will be:

- Effortless
- Precise
- Highly productive

This is the true power of Attract + Action.

To maximize your success using both the Law of Attraction and the Law of Karma, follow these steps:

1. **First, align your thoughts:** Before starting your day, spend ten to fifteen minutes in visualization, affirmations, and meditation. This will set your energy for the day.
2. **Take inspired action:** Once you have clarity, take purposeful and focused action towards your goals.
3. **Trust the process:** Just like a seed takes time to grow into a tree, your actions will bear fruit at the right time.
4. **Keep your vibrations high:** Even if things take time, maintain gratitude and positivity.
5. **Never stop taking action:** The Universe only helps those who help themselves. If you sit idle and only visualize but never act, then no magic will happen.

- Action without the right mindset leads to struggle.
- The right mindset without action leads to nothing.

- But the right mindset + the right action = maximum success.

So, remember this:

1. The Law of Karma tells us to take action.
2. The Law of Attraction tells us to first align ourselves mentally and emotionally.
3. Together, they create the most powerful formula for success!

A person who works with confidence and clarity will achieve in one year what others take ten years to achieve. So, from today, before taking action, first align yourself with the right mindset, belief and energy.

Attract first. Then act. And success will follow.

Day 72

The Law of Attraction as Explained in the Bhagavad Gita

The Bhagavad Gita, one of the most revered scriptures in the world, contained the deepest wisdom on the Law of Attraction long before the modern world gave it this name.

When we talk about the Law of Attraction, we are essentially talking about how our thoughts, beliefs, and actions shape our reality. The Gita explains this concept not just as a belief but as a divine law that governs human life and the Universe itself.

श्रद्धामयोऽयं पुरुषो यो यच्छ्रद्धः स एव सः ॥

'A person is what his faith is. Whatever his faith is, that is what he becomes.'

This verse from Chapter 17, Verse 3, of the Bhagavad Gita clearly states that whatever we believe in and constantly think about, we become.

This is the foundation of the Law of Attraction:

- If you constantly think negatively, you will attract negative situations.

If you constantly think positively, you will attract positive opportunities.

Your faith, beliefs and mindset dictate the reality you experience.

उद्धरेदात्मनात्मानं नात्मानमवसादयेत् ।
आत्मैव ह्यात्मनो बन्धुरात्मैव रिपुरात्मनः ॥

'A person must uplift himself with his own thoughts and not degrade himself. The mind is both his best friend and his worst enemy.'

This verse from Chapter 6, Verse 5, teaches us that our mind is the ultimate force behind our success or failure.

If you use your mind correctly and train it with positive affirmations, visualization and faith, it becomes your best friend, bringing you success, health and prosperity.

However, if you let doubts, fears and negativity take control, your mind becomes your worst enemy and will lead you into a spiral.

ये यथा मां प्रपद्यन्ते तांस्तथैव भजाम्यहम् ।
मम वर्त्मानुवर्तन्ते मनुष्याः पार्थ सर्वशः ॥

As people approach Me, I reciprocate accordingly. All people walk My path in different ways.

This Chapter 4, Verse 11, explains a key truth:

Whatever energy you send out into the Universe, it sends back to you.

- If you approach life with gratitude, love and faith, the Universe will give you abundance, happiness and success.
- If you approach life with fear, doubt and complaints, the Universe will give you struggles and obstacles.

This is why practices such as affirmations, visualization and meditation work—they align your energy with what you want to attract.

अनन्याश्चिन्तयन्तो मां ये जनाः पर्युपासते ।
तेषां नित्याभियुक्तानां योगक्षेमं वहाम्यहम् ॥

To those who are devoted to Me with an undivided mind,
I ensure their well-being and fulfilment of their needs.

This verse from Chapter 9, Verse 22, tells us that when we believe wholeheartedly in the Universe (or God, supreme power, divine intelligence), miracles happen.

This is why faith is the strongest fuel for manifestation!

If you truly believe in your goals, dreams and affirmations without any doubt, the Universe will rearrange itself to make your desires a reality.

सहयज्ञाः प्रजाः सृष्ट्वा पुरोवाच प्रजापतिः ।
अनेन प्रसविष्यध्वमेष वोऽस्त्विष्टकामधुक् ॥

When the Creator made this world, He designed it in a way that those who practise gratitude and selfless service will be blessed abundantly.

This verse from Chapter 3, Verse 10, explains why gratitude is one of the most powerful techniques of the Law of Attraction.

- When you are thankful for what you have, the Universe gives you more.
- If you complain about what you lack, the Universe gives you more struggles.

This is why daily gratitude exercises help in manifesting faster.

1. Your thoughts shape your reality. (Gita 17.3)
2. Train your mind to be your best friend. (Gita 6.5)
3. Detach from outcomes and trust divine timing. (Gita 2.47)
4. You attract energy that matches your vibrations. (Gita 4.11)
5. Faith makes the impossible possible. (Gita 9.22)
6. Gratitude multiplies your blessings. (Gita 3.10)

So, from today, use the Bhagavad Gita's wisdom to master the Law of Attraction!

Whatever you think, so shall you become. Whatever you seek, the Universe will give you. Whatever you act upon with faith, the results shall come.

Keep believing. Keep attracting. Keep growing.

Day 73

Think Like You Already Have It

I have read more than 800 books on success, manifestation and the Law of Attraction. Across all these books, there is one key secret that, if applied correctly, completes the manifestation process and helps you achieve whatever you desire.

Many people take years to understand this concept, but I want to give it to you right now.

Are you ready? Here it is:

Think like you already have it!

1. Why this is the ultimate secret of manifestation

Remember when we discussed affirmations? We always wrote them in the present tense, as if we had already achieved our goals.

- Instead of *I will crack this deal!*
  We wrote *Thank you Universe, for blessing me with success on this deal!*

The Universe responds to your dominant thoughts, emotions and beliefs.

If you think, feel and act like you already have something, your energy aligns with it.

This simple shift in mindset activates the Law of Attraction and makes your manifestation come to life faster.

2. How to apply this in your daily life

If you want career success:

- Walk into your office like you already got the promotion.
- Speak with confidence, as if you're already a leader.

Your belief will make others see you as one.

If you want more sales or business growth:

- Think as if your sales campaign has already been a success.
- Feel the excitement of closing a big deal.

Your mindset shifts your energy, attracting better clients and deals.

If you want to manifest a car:

- Feel like you are already driving it.
- Imagine the steering in your hands, the dashboard, the scent of new leather.

Your subconscious starts working towards making it a reality.

3. The science behind this technique

Your brain cannot distinguish between reality and imagination.

Neuroscientists have found that when you vividly imagine doing something, your brain activates the same neurons as when you actually do it.

This is why Olympic athletes like Michael Phelps (US swimmer) or Neeraj Chopra (Indian javelin thrower) use visualization techniques before competing.

Studies show that basketball players who imagined making free throws improved almost as much as those who physically practised.

4. What stops people from applying this?

I can't think like I already have money when my bank balance is zero. I will believe it when I see it.

The Universe works on the opposite principle: *You will see it when you believe it!*

If you think, feel and act as if you already have it, your reality will adjust to match your thoughts.

5. The key to mastering this principle

For the next seven days, apply this principle in one area of your life.

- If you want confidence, walk, talk and behave as a confident person.
- If you want wealth, start treating yourself with abundance.
- If you want love, start feeling love within yourself first.

Do this consistently and watch how fast things shift in your favour!

You don't manifest what you want. You manifest what you believe you already are.

From today, stop hoping and start believing. Live as if your dreams are already real. And soon, they will be.

Day 74

The Universe's Hidden Answer—a Brain Teaser

Today, let's play a little game. It's simple: I will ask you a question, and I want you to think deeply before you answer.

Ready? Let's begin!

Imagine you are standing in a completely empty room. The walls are plain, and there is nothing inside—no furniture, no windows, no decorations, nothing.

Now, think about the one thing you truly desire the most. It could be a car, a dream job, a relationship, money, success—anything.

Close your eyes for a moment and picture it.

Now, here's the real question:

Where is that thing right now?

If you say, 'It doesn't exist yet,' **you might be wrong.**

Let's uncover the truth together.

Whatever you just wished for ALREADY EXISTS in this world.

Don't believe me? Let me prove it.

At one of my events in Mumbai, I did a small exercise with 500 people in the audience.

I asked one person, 'What do you want?'

His answer: 'I want a Hyundai Creta.'

Then I turned to the audience and said,

'Raise your hand if you already own a Hyundai Creta.'

Three people raised their hands.

Next, I asked someone else, 'What do you desire?'

His answer: 'I want to pass my CA exam and become a chartered accountant.'

Again, I turned to the crowd and asked,

'Who here is already a CA?'

Six or seven hands went up.

What does this tell us?

It proves that whatever you desire ALREADY EXISTS in this world!

- The car you want is already parked in someone's driveway.
- The job you dream of is already held by someone out there.
- The money you seek is already circulating in bank accounts.

So, if it already exists, what does that mean for you?

It means that your dream is NOT impossible. It's simply a matter of bringing it into your own reality.

Science tells us that everything in this universe is energy. Your thoughts, desires and emotions are also energy.

This means that when you desire something, you are tuning in to an energy frequency that already exists.

The mistake most people make: They think their desires are 'far away' or 'difficult to achieve.'

The truth: What you want is already out there. Your job is to align your energy, thoughts and actions so that you can attract it towards you.

From now on, whenever you think *I wish I could have this*, immediately remind yourself:

1. *This already exists. I just need to claim it.*
2. *Someone out there already has it, which means it's 100 per cent possible for me too.*
3. *My job is not to doubt but to align my thoughts and actions towards it.*

The Universe has everything you desire—it's just waiting for you to believe you deserve it.

So, tell me—what is the one thing YOU want? Now, instead of wondering if it's possible, ask yourself:

- Who already has it?
- How can I align my energy to bring it into my life?

Because trust me, it's already there.

Day 75

The Law of Vibration

By now, you have been practising the Law of Attraction for seventy-four days, and you might have noticed something interesting—sometimes it works perfectly, but sometimes it seems like nothing is happening.

If that has ever crossed your mind, then today's lesson is going to change your perspective forever. Because here's the truth:

The Law of Attraction may not work all the time, but the Law of Vibration always does!

Vex King, in his book *Good Vibes, Good Life*, explains this concept beautifully.[22]

- Everything in the Universe is made up of atoms.
- Every atom is constantly vibrating at a certain frequency.
- Your thoughts, emotions and even physical objects all have their own vibrational energy.

What does this mean for us?

If we are in a high vibrational state, we will naturally attract high vibrational things. But if our energy is low, we will attract more low-energy experiences.

⬆ High Vibration Feelings:

- Love
- Gratitude
- Happiness
- Excitement
- Peace
- Inspiration

⬇ Low Vibration Feelings:

- Fear
- Anger
- Jealousy
- Frustration
- Sadness
- Hopelessness

Think about it—have you ever noticed that when you start the day feeling good, everything seems to go smoothly? You find a good parking spot, you get unexpected compliments and your mood stays light.

On the other hand, when you wake up stressed or frustrated, everything starts going wrong—you spill coffee on your clothes, get stuck in traffic, and your entire day feels off.

That is the Law of Vibration at work!

Many people think just repeating affirmations or visualizing success is enough to attract their desires. But if your energy (vibration) is low, your affirmations won't work effectively.

Example:

If you keep saying, 'I am rich', but you actually feel broke, sad or desperate, your vibration is aligned with lack, not wealth.

So, what will you attract? More situations that confirm that lack.

That's why raising your vibration is the key to manifesting anything you want. Want to do it right now? Let's do it!

- **Practise gratitude**—being thankful instantly lifts your energy.
- **Surround yourself with positive people**—energy is contagious.
- **Eat high-vibrational foods**—fresh fruits, vegetables and water boost your body's energy.
- **Move your body**—exercise, dance or even a short walk can increase your energy.
- **Listen to uplifting music**—music has a direct impact on your frequency.
- **Laugh and have fun**—joy is one of the highest vibrational emotions.
- **Meditate**—it clears your mind and raises your vibration effortlessly.

If you only focus on affirmations and visualization but ignore your vibrations, you may struggle to manifest. But if you align your vibrations with what you want, you will naturally attract those things.

So, from today, focus on raising your energy—because when you vibrate high, you attract high!

Day 76

Asking the Universe the Questions That Remain Unanswered

There are moments in life when we find ourselves at a crossroads, unable to make a decision. No matter how much we analyse, think and overthink, the answer doesn't reveal itself.

I've been there too.

I once had to make a life-changing decision:

1. Should I leave my stable job and permanently switch to public speaking and corporate training, which I was being offered?
2. Or should I stick to my job and aim for growth within the corporate world?

It was a tough choice, one that could impact the rest of my life.

Today, you all know what I chose. I stand in front of you, speaking, teaching and sharing my journey. But what you don't know is how I made this decision.

I was stuck, uncertain about which path to take. So, I did something different—something that I now want to share with you.

That night, before sleeping, I asked the Universe for guidance.

I kept thinking about my question: *What should I do? Should I leave my job and follow my passion, or should I stay?*

I focused on this question until I fell asleep, allowing it to settle deep into my subconscious mind.

The next morning, something incredible happened. Within twenty-four hours, I received two offers for corporate training—without even applying for them!

That was my answer.

The Universe had responded.

That day, I realized a powerful truth—when you don't have the answer, the Universe will guide you. You just need to ask.

Step 1: Before going to sleep, focus on the question that is troubling you.

Step 2: Keep thinking about it until it gets embedded into your subconscious mind.

Step 3: Let it go and sleep. Do not force an answer.

Step 4: Be open to receiving the answer the next day—it can come as a thought, an idea, a person's advice or even an unexpected event.

The subconscious mind works closely with the Universe. When you focus on a question before sleeping, your subconscious starts looking for an answer—not just in your mind, but in the world around you.

This is the Law of Attraction at work. Your thoughts are energy, and when you put out the energy of a question, the Universe aligns the right answers for you.

If you are stuck in life and don't know what to do, ask the Universe. The answer will come—sometimes in a dream, sometimes in a conversation, sometimes through an unexpected opportunity.

Just be open to receiving it.

Tonight, try this. Ask the Universe a question and see what happens next.

Day 77

What Is Your Frequency?

I have an important question for you today.

What is your frequency?

Take a moment to pause and reflect.

People often ask me:

'Why am I facing so many hardships?'

'Why is my life so difficult compared to others?'

'If God is truly almighty, why am I being treated unfairly?'

To those who ask these questions, I respond with another question:

Have you ever stopped to check your own frequency?

Your frequency = your reality

Remember when we discussed the Law of Vibrations?

1. Everything in this Universe is made up of energy.
2. Every person, every thought and every event carries a vibrational frequency.

3. What you emit, you attract—it's that simple.

Now, ask yourself:

- Are you constantly stressed, angry, doubtful or frustrated?
- Do you find yourself complaining more than appreciating?
- Do you focus on what's missing instead of what's available?

If your answer is yes, then your frequency is low, and that is exactly what you are attracting—more struggles, more delays, more disappointments.

The Universe does not punish anyone, nor does it reward anyone unfairly.

It simply mirrors what you are projecting into it.

- If you are calm, grateful, joyful and hopeful → your frequency is high.
  If you are frustrated, doubtful, angry or complaining → your frequency is low.

What you attract is determined by your current energy.

So, if you are experiencing difficulties, it may not be because God is unfair—it might be because you are stuck in a negative loop.

Step 1: Awareness → Acknowledge that your energy is shaping your life.

Step 2: Shift your focus → Move from what's wrong to what's right.

Step 3: Gratitude practice → Every day, appreciate at least *five* things in your life.

Step 4: Reduce negativity → Avoid toxic people, negative conversations and unnecessary stress.

Step 5: Engage in high-vibration activities → Exercise, meditate, listen to uplifting music or spend time in nature.

Now, make a conscious effort to radiate positive energy every day and watch how the Universe responds!

Day 78

The Cold, Hard Truth—You Created Everything in Your Life

Today, I'm going to tell you something that might be difficult to accept, but once you do, it will change your life forever.

Everything happening in your life right now:

- The good moments
- The bad moments
- The struggles, the successes, the delays, the achievements

It was all created by you.

Yes, you created it. Your thoughts, your beliefs, your choices, your actions and your energy— they all shaped your current reality.

Now, before you jump to say, 'But I never asked for struggles!' let's break this down logically and truthfully.

Everything in this world operates on energy and vibration.

- When you repeatedly focus on fears, doubts and struggles → you attract more of them.
- When you make decisions based on insecurity → you limit your opportunities.
- When you complain about life → you signal the Universe that you enjoy complaining, so it gives you more reasons to complain.
- When you refuse to take action → the Universe assumes you are comfortable where you are, so it doesn't push you towards your dreams.

Now, here's the liberating part of this truth:

You have created everything in your life, but you also have the power to UNCREATE it.

You are not stuck. You are not helpless. You are not destined to struggle forever.

If you accept that you created your hardships through your past thoughts and actions, then you can also change your thoughts and actions to build a different future.

1. Take 100 per cent responsibility

- Stop blaming people, luck, circumstances or destiny.
- Look in the mirror and accept it: *I created this*.

2. Identify the thought patterns that led here

- Ask yourself: What were my dominant thoughts in the past five years?
- Were they filled with doubts, fears, complaints or limitations?

- What beliefs did I hold about money, relationships, health and success?

3. Shift to empowering thoughts

- If you believed *Money is hard to earn*, change it to *Money flows to me easily*.
- If you believed *I am unlucky in relationships*, change it to *I attract love and joy effortlessly*.

4. Take new actions that support your desires

- If you want success, start acting like a successful person.
- If you want love, start giving love instead of waiting for it.
- If you want health, start prioritizing your well-being.

Write down three things in your life that you don't like. Then, ask yourself:

How did my past thoughts, actions and beliefs contribute to these?

Now, write a *new* belief that will help you uncreate these situations.

If you fully embrace this truth today, your life will never be the same.

Starting *now*, take back control. Recreate your reality with intention, positivity and action.

Day 79

The Secret to Receiving—Gratitude in Advance

Let me ask you something.

When you go to the temple, sit for prayer or close your eyes to speak to God, what's the first thing you say?

Most people say:

- 'Please help me get that job.'
- 'Please solve this problem.'
- 'Please bless me with a good partner.'

But today, I want to introduce you to a secret that will change how you manifest forever.

The most powerful way to bring something into your life . . . *is by being grateful for it before it even shows up.*

Let's say that again: **Be grateful *in advance*.**

This isn't just positive thinking. This is a higher vibration—a powerful energy that tells the Universe:

I already believe. I already know it's mine.

Think about it: **Would you doubt something you *already* had?**

That's the point. The moment you show gratitude for your desire as if it's already yours, you collapse the time it takes for the Universe to deliver it.

Why does this work?

Because you're no longer coming from a place of lack or desperation. You're coming from **faith, certainty** and **alignment**.

Let's take a few examples:

Instead of saying, 'Please, God, help me get that dream job', say:

Thank you, Universe, for my dream job. It fits me perfectly, and I enjoy every moment of it.

Instead of 'I wish I had a loving partner', say:

Thank you, God, for the beautiful relationship I'm in. I feel so loved and respected every day.

Instead of 'I really need more money,' say:

Thank you, Universe, for the financial abundance that keeps flowing into my life. I am so blessed.

Feel the shift in energy? That's the magic.

Now here's your task for today:

Gratitude in advance practice

1. Close your eyes and take five deep breaths.
2. Now, visualize one of your biggest desires.
3. Imagine it has already happened—how do you feel?
4. Say *thank you* in as many ways as you can.
5. Write down **five things you're grateful for in advance**, like this:

- *Thank you, Universe, for the beautiful house I now live in.*
- *Thank you for my vibrant health and boundless energy.*
- *Thank you, God, for my dream vacation that felt like a miracle.*
- *Thank you for the growth and success in my business.*
- *Thank you for the joy and harmony in my family life.*

Every time you pray or talk to the Universe from now on, try this.

When you believe something is already yours, the Universe has no choice but to **match your energy** and **deliver** it.

You don't have to chase your dreams. You just have to **receive** them.

And gratitude in advance is how you open the door.

Day 80

The Placebo Effect—the Science Behind Manifestation

Did you know that your mind has the power to heal your body? Have you ever heard of people recovering from illnesses simply because they *believed* they would? This isn't just a miracle—it's a scientifically studied phenomenon called the placebo effect, and it beautifully aligns with the Law of Attraction.

We've spent the last seventy-nine days understanding how our thoughts, beliefs and emotions shape our reality. But today, we are diving into a powerful truth: *Your mind can directly impact your body and your life.*

In simple terms, the placebo effect happens when a person experiences real improvements in their health after taking a treatment that has no actual medical effect—just because they *believe* it will work.

Doctors and researchers have studied this effect for decades. In countless medical trials, patients who were given sugar pills (placebos) instead of real medicine showed significant improvements in their conditions. How? Because their minds were convinced that they were receiving real treatment, and their bodies *responded accordingly*.

This is the same mechanism that the Law of Attraction operates on. The energy of belief and expectation creates real, tangible effects.

The Law of Attraction states that *whatever we believe in, we attract*. The placebo effect proves this.

- When patients believe they are healing, their bodies respond and actually begin to heal.
- When you believe you are wealthy, opportunities for wealth begin appearing in your life.
- When you believe you are successful, you start acting in ways that bring success closer to you.

The mind is so powerful that it tricks the body into creating reality—whether that is healing, success or abundance. The Universe is always responding to what we truly believe.

Studies have shown that the placebo effect is not just in the mind—it has measurable biological effects. Scientists have recorded that when a patient expects pain relief, the brain releases endorphins, the body's natural painkillers. When a person expects recovery, the immune system boosts its healing response.

Now, let's apply this understanding to our lives. If simply believing in a pill can heal a person, imagine what believing in *yourself* can do!

The placebo effect teaches us that belief alone can shape reality. Here's how you can use this knowledge in your Law of Attraction journey:

1. **Believe in your desires as if they are already achieved.**
    Just like patients believe they are healing, you must believe you already have what you are manifesting. Don't just hope—*know* that it's coming.

2. **Remove doubt from your mind.**
    The placebo effect fails when a patient doubts the treatment. Similarly, if you doubt the process of manifestation, you disrupt the energy flow. Replace doubts with certainty.

3. **Embrace positive expectations.**
    Your thoughts are powerful signals. Expect miracles, expect success, expect abundance—and watch the Universe respond.

The placebo effect is scientific proof that your mind is far more powerful than you think. What you believe, you receive.

The real question is: *What are you believing in?* Are you focusing on lack, or are you focusing on abundance? Are you doubting, or are you trusting?

It's time to take charge of your beliefs. Just like the placebo effect heals the body, the Law of Attraction heals your life.

Day 81

Dream Big—The Universe Is Listening

Have you ever stopped yourself from dreaming big? Have you ever hesitated before setting a goal because a little voice inside you whispered:

- *What if I fail?*
- *What if it's too difficult?*
- *What if I am being selfish?*
- *What if it is out of my league?*

These thoughts don't just hold you back; they chain you down.

The truth is, if you don't allow yourself to dream big, you limit what the Universe can give you.

A lot of people fear dreaming big because they don't want to be disappointed. Others think that dreaming big is unrealistic or that they should only wish for things that seem 'practical' or 'achievable'.

But here's the truth: The only limitations that exist are the ones you create in your own mind.

If you tell yourself that you can't have something, you automatically shut the door to that possibility. But if you believe that *anything is possible*, the Universe aligns itself to make it happen.

Many people say, 'I will just keep working hard, and success will come on its own.' That is half true.

Yes, the Law of Karma rewards effort. If you put in hard work, you will see results. But the question is:

How far will it take you?

If you never dream beyond what seems 'safe', your hard work will only take you to a limited destination. But if you dream beyond your limits, your actions and efforts will take you beyond what you ever imagined.

Dreaming big is like giving the Universe a blueprint of your desires. It tells the Universe, *This is what I want. This is what I am working towards.*

If you want to manifest your biggest desires, follow these steps:

1. **Give yourself permission to dream big.**
   - Stop thinking about what is 'realistic'. Your dreams don't have to make sense to anyone else. They are your dreams.

2. **Believe you deserve it.**
   - You can only manifest what you truly believe you can have.
   - If you don't believe in yourself, the Universe won't believe in you either.

Dreaming big is not selfish. It is not impossible. It is not foolish.

It is necessary.

The Universe listens to those who dare to dream beyond their limits.

So, today, allow yourself to dream without fear. Visualize the life you want without limitations. Because the moment you start believing in the impossible, the Universe starts making it possible.

Day 82

Must-Follow Health Affirmations for Perfect Health

Hey there, I hope you are doing well. You see, today we are going to discuss another cool technique that will help you in a way that everyone wants help in.

But first, you need to realize something. For that, sit at your regular spot, focus and relax.

Are you at your fixed spot? Great, now follow my lead.

Sit back. Close your eyes.

Feel your body. Feel the air moving in and out of your lungs. Feel the rhythm of your heart. Your body is working for you every second of every day.

How do you feel in this moment? Are you aware of the magic within you?

Take a deep breath and focus on the life force flowing through your body. You are alive. You are well.

If you are feeling unwell right now, believe this: your body is healing. You are becoming stronger. Every cell of your body is working to restore balance.

Your body responds to your thoughts. The Law of Attraction applies to your health just as much as it does to your dreams.

Have you ever noticed how stress and negativity make you feel physically weak? Or how happiness makes you feel lighter, more energetic and full of life?

This is because your thoughts create energy within your body. When you affirm good health, your body aligns itself with that positive energy, and healing takes place faster.

The secret? Train your mind to believe you are healthy, and your body will follow.

Today, I give you ten affirmations for perfect health.

Your task: Stand in front of a mirror every morning, look into your own eyes and repeat these affirmations aloud. Let them sink deep into your subconscious.

1. All is well.
2. I am well.
3. My body is well.
4. I am healthy, healthy, healthy.
5. Thank you for my body's perfect health.
6. I am in great shape; I am fit and well.
7. I am a picture of good health.
8. My body is in perfect balance and perfect health.
9. My body is 100 per cent perfectly well.
10. I am manifesting perfect stability in my body.

Scientific research has shown that positive thoughts and affirmations reduce stress, enhance immune function and speed up recovery.

Dr Masaru Emoto's studies on water molecules proved that positive words and emotions create beautiful, harmonious structures, while negative emotions create chaotic, distorted patterns.[23] Your body is 70 per cent water, so imagine the effect of affirming health every single day!

From this moment, commit to your health.

Every day, visualize yourself in perfect health. See yourself full of energy, glowing with vitality. Feel gratitude for your body and all that it does for you.

Your body is your greatest ally; treat it with love, and it will respond with well-being, strength, and perfect health.

Day 83

Think and Grow Rich—The Mindset of Wealth

'Whatever the mind can conceive and believe, it can achieve.'—Napoleon Hill

You've likely heard of *Think and Grow Rich*, one of the most influential books on success and wealth creation. But have you ever wondered why this book is so powerful?

What makes *Think and Grow Rich* unique is that it's not just about money—it's about reprogramming your mind for abundance. If you've been following this book closely, you'll realize that Napoleon Hill's teachings align perfectly with the Law of Attraction.

Today, we are diving deep into how *Think and Grow Rich* can help you attract wealth, success and prosperity into your life using the exact same principles we have been practising.

Napoleon Hill spent over twenty-five years studying 500 of the most successful people in the world—

including Henry Ford, Thomas Edison and Andrew Carnegie. After decades of research, he discovered that wealth and success are not just about hard work; they are about mindset.

His conclusion? The thoughts you hold in your mind shape your reality.

This is exactly what we have been practising with the Law of Attraction.

Hill emphasized that success is built on the definite nature of purpose, belief and action. This means:

1. You must have a clear goal (**clarity**).
2. You must believe it is possible for you (**faith**).
3. You must take action towards it (**aligned action**).

Napoleon Hill describes **six powerful principles** that directly connect with the Law of Attraction. Let's see how they work:

1. Burning desire: the starting point of all success

Hill explains that every great achievement starts with a burning desire.

- You don't just 'wish' for something. You must want it so badly that it consumes your thoughts.
- The Law of Attraction works the same way: the stronger your desire, the more powerful your manifestation.
- Ask yourself: How strong is my desire? If it's weak, it won't manifest.

Action: Write down your goal and read it aloud every morning and night.

2. Faith: believing in the invisible

Hill says that faith is the foundation of riches. If you doubt yourself or your ability to attract wealth, you won't succeed.

- This is exactly what we have discussed in the Law of Attraction.
- If you don't believe you deserve money, how will you attract it?

Action: Replace negative thoughts about money with positive affirmations.

Example: Instead of saying 'I don't have enough money', say *Money flows easily and abundantly to me.*

3. Autosuggestion: programming your subconscious mind

Autosuggestion is another word for affirmations! Hill taught that your subconscious mind accepts whatever you repeatedly tell it.

- We have already discussed this in the 10x3 Affirmation Method and Scripting Method.
- The more you repeat and feel your affirmations, the more they become your reality.

 # Action: Every day, write and say your money affirmations with emotion.

4. Specialized knowledge: the power of learning

Hill explains that successful people never stop learning.

- The Universe rewards those who expand their knowledge and develop their skills.
- If you want financial success, start learning about money, business and wealth-building strategies.

 # Action: Make a habit of reading books about wealth and success.

5. Decision: removing indecisiveness

One of the biggest reasons people fail is indecision.

- The Universe cannot send you opportunities if you keep changing your mind.
- The Law of Attraction works when you commit fully to your goal.

 # Action: Decide what you want and stick to it. No second-guessing.

6. Persistence: the key to manifestation

Napoleon Hill says that persistence is the #1 reason people succeed.

- Many people quit right before their manifestation is about to happen.
- Just like we discussed in Divine Timing, the Universe has its own schedule.

Action: Stay consistent. Even if you don't see results immediately, keep going!

Think and Grow Rich is not just a book; it is a proven system for transforming your mindset.

If you apply these principles alongside your Law of Attraction practices, you will attract the wealth and success you desire.

Remember, *you are one thought away from changing your financial reality. Start thinking like a rich person, and soon, you will be one!*

Day 84

Fighting Stress with the Law of Attraction

Before we begin today's lesson, I want you to take a deep breath. Hold it for three seconds . . . and release. Now, do this three more times.

How do you feel? A little lighter? A little more present?

Stress, anxiety and depression can feel overwhelming. But today, we are going to take a stand. If you have ever felt like stress is controlling you, today is the day you take back control.

It's time to use the Law of Attraction to transform stress into peace, doubt into faith and fear into confidence.

Step 1: Have faith in yourself.

One of the biggest reasons stress takes over is because we lose faith in ourselves. We start questioning if we are capable, if we will succeed or if things will ever get better.

But let me tell you a secret: your subconscious mind is more powerful than you realize.

Your subconscious already knows how to heal you. It knows how to bring success, happiness and peace into your life. All you need to do is trust it and feed it the right messages.

Action step: Every morning, stand in front of the mirror, look yourself in the eye, and say:

*I trust myself. My subconscious mind is powerful, and
I am capable of handling anything that comes my way.*

Say it with conviction. Feel it. This one habit will start changing your inner world.

Step 2: Visualize your future self.

Now, close your eyes for a moment. Imagine the version of yourself that is completely stress free. The version of you that has achieved everything you desire.

What does this version of you look like?

What do they feel like?

How do they wake up in the morning?

How do they talk, walk and live?

If you keep visualizing your best self every day, your mind will start working towards making it real.

Did you know that Olympic athletes use visualization techniques before their competitions? They mentally rehearse their wins, which actually improves their performance in real life.

So, if visualization can make athletes win medals, imagine what it can do for your life.

Action step: Every night before you sleep, visualize your future self as if you have already become that person. Picture every detail, and let yourself feel the excitement.

Step 3: Use subliminal messages to reprogramme your mind.

Your brain is constantly absorbing the messages you give it. If you keep repeating negative thoughts like

- *I am so stressed.*
- *Nothing is working out for me.*
- *I am stuck.*

Your subconscious accepts these as truth and makes sure your life reflects them.

But what happens when you change these thoughts into positive affirmations?

- *I am calm, strong and in control of my emotions.*
- *Everything is working in my favour.*
- *My life is filled with peace and abundance.*

Your mind starts working towards making these statements real.

Action step: Write down your favourite positive affirmations. Record yourself saying them and add soft, relaxing music in the background. Listen to them every morning and night.

Your subconscious will absorb them while you sleep and start shifting your energy towards positivity.

Stress is temporary, but the strength within you is permanent. The more you train your mind to focus on peace and positivity, the less control stress will have over you.

You are in control of your energy. You are powerful. And today, you take the first step towards living a stress-free, fulfilling life.

Are you ready? Then start right now.

Day 85

How Effective Are Your Law of Attraction Practices?

For the past **eighty-four** days, you have been practising various Law of Attraction techniques: affirmations, visualization, mirror techniques, subliminal messages, writing exercises and more. But have you ever wondered which technique is the most effective?

How much of what you are practising actually engraves itself into your subconscious mind?

Today, we will break down the effectiveness of each method so that you can maximize your results and strengthen your manifestations.

Your subconscious mind absorbs information through repetition and emotional impact. Studies in cognitive psychology have shown that the more senses you engage while learning or practising something, the deeper it imprints into your subconscious.

This is why some techniques are far more powerful than others. Let's analyse them one by one:

1. **Typing affirmations—10 per cent retention**
   Many people prefer typing affirmations on their phone or laptop, but the impact is minimal. Typing is passive, meaning your mind is not fully engaged. It's better than doing nothing, but it does not create a deep impact.

2. **Reading affirmations—20 per cent retention**
   Reading affirmations aloud helps a little more because your mind processes the words, but it is still passive. If you read without feeling emotion, your subconscious won't absorb much of it.

3. **Listening to subliminal messages—30 per cent retention**
   Subliminal messages are affirmations embedded in music or recordings. This technique gradually reprogrammes the subconscious mind over time, especially when used during sleep. While effective, it works best when combined with other practices rather than as a standalone technique.

4. **Speaking affirmations (mirror technique)—50 per cent retention**
   When you speak affirmations out loud, especially while looking into a mirror, it creates a powerful emotional connection. You are hearing yourself believe in your desires, and your subconscious mind absorbs the confidence in your voice.

5. **Visualization—75 per cent retention**
   Visualization is one of the most powerful Law of
   Attraction techniques. Why? Because your mind
   cannot tell the difference between reality and a
   vividly imagined scenario. When you visualize with
   full emotions, senses, and clarity, your subconscious
   accepts it as truth, accelerating manifestation.

6. **Writing affirmations—100 per cent retention**
   Writing is the most effective technique because it
   activates both physical and mental energy. Studies
   show that when you write something down, your
   brain processes it more deeply than when you just
   read or say it. This is why journaling and scripting
   affirmations are the most powerful ways to imprint
   desires into your subconscious.

- Engages the mind and body: when you write, you
  involve physical movement, which deepens neural
  pathways in your brain. When you visualize, your
  brain experiences your goal as if it's already real.
- Creates emotional connection: writing your desires
  down forces you to focus and think about them.
  Visualization allows you to experience the emotions
  of already having them.
- Strengthens belief and clarity: writing and visualization
  provide clarity about what you want. When you are
  clear, the Universe responds faster.

Scientific fact: According to Dr Gail Matthews from
Dominican University, people who write down their goals

are 42 per cent more likely to achieve them compared to those who don't.[24]

Your daily Law of Attraction routine should include:

Writing affirmations daily to deeply engrave them into your subconscious.

Visualizing your success with full emotions and details every morning and night.

Speaking affirmations out loud while looking in the mirror.

If you have been only reading or typing affirmations, it's time to level up your practice and shift to writing and visualization for faster and stronger results!

By now, you understand that not all Law of Attraction techniques are equal. Some create faster subconscious shifts, while others work gradually over time.

Now, take a moment and ask yourself, *Which of these techniques have I been using the most*?

If you want rapid and powerful results, prioritize writing and visualization daily. The Universe is always listening, but how clearly and deeply you communicate with it depends on the techniques you choose.

Let's take your manifestation journey to the next level!

Day 86

Decoding Angel Numbers—Signs from the Universe

Have you ever noticed repeating numbers like **111, 222, 333, 444** on clocks, licence plates, receipts or phone numbers?

Have you ever felt like certain numbers keep appearing to you over and over again?

If yes, then congratulations! You have been receiving divine signs from the Universe.

These numbers are called **Angel Numbers,** and they carry powerful messages about your life, energy and the path you are walking.

Angel numbers are sequences of numbers that repeatedly appear in your life as a way for the Universe, God or your spiritual guides to communicate with you. They serve as guidance, confirmations and reminders that you are on the right track or that certain changes are necessary.

These numbers are not coincidences; they are synchronicities—special patterns that are meant to grab your attention.

In the Law of Attraction, angel numbers act as signals that your manifestations are working. They validate your energy, reminding you to stay focused, aligned and positive.

When you see angel numbers, it means the Universe is responding to your vibrations.

Think of them as green lights on your manifestation journey—assuring you that you are moving in the right direction.

Each angel number carries a specific meaning. Here's a basic breakdown:

111: New beginnings and manifestation

You are entering a powerful phase where your thoughts are turning into reality.

Stay positive and focus only on what you want, not on what you fear.

222: Balance and alignment

A sign that your life is coming into harmony. Keep trusting the process—your manifestations are unfolding.

333: Creativity and divine support

The Universe is guiding you towards expansion, creativity and personal growth. Trust that your dreams are being supported.

444: Protection and stability

A sign that your angels and guides are surrounding you with protection.

Keep working towards your dreams; you are being supported.

555: Transformation and change

Big life changes are on the way—embrace them! The Universe is shifting things for your highest good.

777: Spiritual awakening and luck

You are evolving spiritually and aligning with your true purpose. A sign that your manifestations are close to becoming reality.

888: Abundance and success

Financial and personal abundance is on its way. Stay focused, and don't let doubts hold you back.

999: Closure and new beginnings

Something in your life is completing, making space for something new. Embrace endings as stepping stones to new blessings.

000: Divine connection and infinite possibilities.

This is the number of *pure potential*. It represents the presence of the divine in your life and the infinite nature of the Universe.

Now that you know what these numbers mean, how can you use them to boost your manifestations?

1. Acknowledge the signs with gratitude.

When you see an angel number, pause, smile, and say, 'Thank you, Universe'.

This strengthens your connection with divine energy.

2. Reflect on what you were thinking about.

Angel numbers often appear when your thoughts match their meaning. If you see 111 while thinking about a dream job, it means you are manifesting it!

3. Take inspired action.

These numbers encourage you to act. If 555 appears and you've been hesitant to make a big decision, it's a sign to move forward.

4. Keep your energy high.

Angel numbers are a reminder to stay positive, trust the process and align with abundance.

Whenever you see angel numbers, celebrate them! They are proof that the Universe is listening and responding to you.

So, the next time you see repeating numbers, take a deep breath, trust the message and keep moving forward. The Universe has your back!

Your manifestations are on their way—just keep believing!

Day 87

Rewiring Your Brain for a Better Life

Have you ever felt like no matter what you do, things just don't seem to work out? Do you ever feel stuck in patterns of negativity, self-doubt or just a general sense that life isn't going your way?

If yes, then today is one of the most important lessons in your journey with the Law of Attraction.

You see, the way you think and act every day determines what you attract in life. Your brain is a machine of patterns, and most of us have trained it to run on autopilot—unconsciously repeating the same emotions, thoughts and actions that keep us stuck in the same situations.

But here's the good news: you can rewire your brain.

And today, I am giving you a simple yet powerful three-step practice that will help you reset your thinking, break old patterns and attract better energy into your life.

Starting today, follow these three simple actions every morning for the next ten days.

Step 1: Change your dominant hand while brushing your teeth.

- If you usually brush your teeth with your right hand, use your left hand instead (or vice versa).
- At first, this will feel strange, uncomfortable or even frustrating. That's the point.
- This small change forces your brain to wake up, become more conscious and break old, repetitive patterns.

Why does this work?

Changing small daily habits creates new neural pathways in your brain. Research in neuroplasticity (the brain's ability to rewire itself) has shown that doing things differently increases mental flexibility and improves your ability to break negative cycles.

Brain Fact: A study in the journal *Nature Neuroscience* found that doing simple activities differently every day can improve focus, memory and creativity.

Step 2: Stand in front of a mirror and say 'I love you' ten times.

- Look into your own eyes.
- Say 'I love you' out loud ten times.
- Feel it. Mean it. Even if it feels weird or forced at first, keep going.

Why does this work?

Most people struggle with self-love. If you have been criticizing yourself, doubting yourself or feeling unworthy, you are sending negative vibrations into the Universe.

When you practise self-love, you shift your energy. You send a new message to your subconscious mind:

I am worthy. I deserve love. I deserve success.

Mirror work is a technique taught by Louise Hay, a world-renowned self-help teacher.[25] She found that speaking positive affirmations to your reflection directly impacts your subconscious mind and increases self-confidence.

Step 3: Do twenty-five cycles of exaggerated deep breathing.

- Stand tall, take a deep exaggerated breath and fill your lungs completely.
- Exhale fully.
- Repeat this for twenty-five cycles.

Why does this work?

Breathing exercises activate the parasympathetic nervous system, which reduces stress, anxiety and negative thoughts.

Most of us breathe shallowly, keeping our body in a state of low energy and mental fog. By taking deliberate deep breaths, we clear our mind and recharge our energy field.

Scientific fact: Studies show that controlled breathing reduces cortisol (the stress hormone) and improves emotional regulation. This means you'll feel more in control of your thoughts, emotions and actions.

I challenge you to commit to these three simple actions every morning for ten days.

What will happen?

- Your brain will become more flexible—breaking old patterns of negativity.
- You will develop more self-love and confidence.
- Your thoughts will become clearer and more positive.
- You will naturally start attracting better things in life.

This is a small but powerful way to reset your mind, align with the Law of Attraction, and open the doors to new opportunities.

Start today. The change you seek begins with one simple decision.

Day 88

The Power of Words—Never Speak Against Yourself

'Do not allow negative thoughts to enter your mind, for they are the weeds that strangle confidence.'—Bruce Lee

Bruce Lee was known for his wisdom just as much as his physical mastery. There is one particular lesson he taught that is extremely relevant to the Law of Attraction and self-belief.

He once said:

'Do not say anything negative about yourself, even as a joke. Your body doesn't know the difference. Words are energy, and they cast spells; that's why it's called spelling. Change the way you speak about yourself, and you can change your life.'

Take a moment to reflect. How do you speak about yourself?

- Do you casually say, 'I am so unlucky' or 'I always fail at this?'
- Do you say, 'I am terrible at remembering things' or 'I can never lose weight?'

If so, today is the day you stop doing that.

There is an ancient story about a tribe in a distant land that never cuts trees. Instead, when they need to remove a tree, they surround it and begin to curse it, insult it and speak negative words to it every single day.

What happens?

After some time, the tree begins to rot from the inside. Eventually, it falls on its own.

Now, let's apply this to you.

If constant negativity can kill a tree, imagine what it can do to your mind, body and soul when you speak negatively about yourself.

Your words have energy. When you insult yourself, even jokingly, you plant seeds of self-doubt and weakness inside your subconscious mind.

Your subconscious mind does not understand jokes—it takes everything literally. So, every time you say something negative about yourself, you programme your mind to believe it.

Modern psychology confirms that repeating statements about yourself rewires your brain.

- If you constantly say 'I can never do this', your brain creates pathways of self-doubt.
- If you say 'I am getting better every day', your brain believes it and works towards it.

From today onwards, change how you speak about yourself.

Stop saying:

- *I always mess things up.*
- *I am so unlucky.*
- *I am not good enough.*
- *I don't deserve success.*

Instead, say:

- *I always find solutions.*
- *Good things come my way.*
- *I am constantly improving.*
- *I am deserving of all good things.*

Your words are like seeds—whatever you plant, you will harvest. Speak powerfully and positively about yourself and watch how your life transforms.

The Universe listens to everything you say. So, choose your words wisely.

Day 89

How to Live a Positive Life Every Day

Take a moment and ask yourself: How many thoughts do you think you have in a single day?

50,000? 60,000? Or maybe even more?

For years, studies have estimated that we have around 60,000 thoughts per day, but recent research suggests the number is closer to 6000 thoughts daily. Now, here's the real kicker—80 per cent of those thoughts tend to be negative, and 95 per cent of them are repetitive.

That means, unless you are consciously shifting your focus, your brain is running on autopilot, feeding you the same old worries, fears and doubts over and over again.

Now, here's the question:

How do we break free from this cycle and start living a positive life?

The answer is simple—you must take charge of your thoughts.

By now, if you've been following our daily exercises, especially the morning routine from Day 50, you should already be feeling a shift in your energy.

You might be feeling lighter, happier, or simply more in control of your life.

But if you still feel stuck, don't worry. Today, I am giving you the key to maintaining a positive life:

Your mindset determines how you process your reality.

Your life is not about what happens to you.

Your life is about how you respond to what happens to you.

The problem is, most people allow their negative thoughts to overpower their positive ones. But the truth is, you can train your brain to focus on the positive and rewire it for success.

To truly live a positive life, you must focus on three core practices:

1. Follow the Law of Attraction daily practices.

Remember when we spoke about the importance of affirmations and visualizations?

These aren't just feel-good activities—they are tools to help condition your subconscious mind for positivity.

- **Affirmations:** The words you say to yourself every day create your reality. If you affirm success, you attract success. If you affirm struggle, you attract struggle.
- **Visualization:** Your brain cannot distinguish between reality and a vividly imagined scenario. The more you visualize positive outcomes, the more your mind starts believing in them.

The more you repeat positive thoughts, the more your subconscious absorbs them and begins to create a new reality for you.

2. Shift your focus from negative to positive.

Negative thoughts will always exist, but you get to choose what you focus on.

Let's do a quick exercise:

Think about the last time you were in a bad mood.

Maybe someone cut you off in traffic, or you had a frustrating conversation.

What happened after that? Chances are, your entire day felt worse because you focused on that one negative moment.

Now, let's reverse it.

Think about the last time you felt truly happy.

Maybe you heard some good news or a stranger smiled at you or you received a small unexpected gift.

What happened after that? Your energy shifted to a higher vibration, and suddenly, your day seemed brighter.

What changed? Only your focus.

If you train your mind to focus on the good, the good will expand in your life.

3. Reduce negative thought patterns.

Negative thoughts aren't the problem—the problem is when we engage with them and give them power.

So, how do we reduce them?

- **Challenge your thoughts:**
  Whenever a negative thought appears, pause and ask yourself:
  'Is this thought really true?'
  Most of the time, negative thoughts are just fears and assumptions, not reality.

- **Use a mental filter:**
  Whenever something happens, try to find at least one good thing about it.
  Even the worst situations have lessons to teach us.

- **Practise gratitude:**
  Gratitude is the ultimate tool to shift from negativity to positivity.
  When you focus on what you already have, you stop stressing over what you don't.

From today onwards, I want you to become aware of your thoughts.

- Keep a journal and write down five positive things that happened each day.
- Every time you catch yourself thinking negatively, replace it with a positive thought.
- Start your morning with affirmations and end your day with gratitude.

By doing this consistently, your mind will automatically start filtering out negativity and focusing on positivity.

Remember, you don't need to eliminate negative thoughts completely—you just need to stop feeding them.

Your energy flows where your attention goes.

So, from today, feed your positivity and watch how your life transforms.

Let's make every thought count!

Day 90

What Do You Get When You Have an Orange?

Let's start today with a simple question:

What do you get when you have an orange?

Think about it for a second. What's your answer? Orange juice? Maybe the fruit itself? Hold onto that thought because the answer may shock you.

Before we get to it, let's dive into today's discussion.

There is a profound teaching in the Bhagavad Gita that resonates deeply with today's topic:

'चित्तस्य शुद्धये कर्म, न तु वस्तूपलब्धये।'

(*Chittasya Shuddhaye Karma, Na Tu Vastupalabdhaye.*)

Actions are performed to purify the mind, not merely to attain material results.

This means that whatever is inside you—your emotions, your mindset, your energy—is what will reflect in your actions and reactions in daily life.

Think about it. When you squeeze an orange, what comes out? *Orange juice*. Not apple juice. Not mango juice. Just orange juice. Why? Because that's what's inside it.

Now, let's apply this concept to ourselves.

Let's say you're in a tough situation:

- You're stuck in traffic, running late for an important meeting.
- Someone criticizes you unfairly.
- A plan you worked hard on suddenly falls apart.

How do you react?

For most people, what's inside them is what spills out in difficult moments.

- If you are filled with anger, you lash out.
- If you are filled with stress, you panic and make mistakes.
- If you are filled with frustration, you blame others or complain.
- If you are filled with self-doubt, you give up.

But what if you had something different inside you?

- If you are filled with calmness, you stay composed.
- If you are filled with gratitude, you see lessons in failures.

🔘 If you are filled with confidence, you tackle challenges head-on.

🔘 If you are filled with positivity, you uplift yourself and others.

The reality is that life will always squeeze you—through hardships, stress, unexpected events and obstacles. What comes out of you depends on what's already inside you.

If you want to react positively in difficult situations, you have to fill yourself with positivity every day.

We have been following this in parts every day unconsciously. See, the practices we use for the Law of Attraction are so intertwined with your inherent living being that they give you side benefits that you are not even hoping to achieve. But if you want to follow this consciously, here is how we do it:

1. **Start your day with gratitude.** The more you focus on what's good, the more good things you attract.
2. **Feed your mind with positivity.** Read uplifting books, listen to motivational talks and surround yourself with positive people.
3. **Practise self-awareness.** The next time you feel triggered, pause and ask: *What am I holding inside that is making me react this way?*
4. **Let go of past negativity.** If you carry resentment, frustration, or stress inside you, that's what will come out when pressure is applied. Learn to release it.
5. **Stay mindful.** Meditate, practise deep breathing and keep your mind centred on solutions rather than problems.

Now, let's go back to our question:

What do you get when you have an orange?

The answer? You get orange juice.

Not because you want it, but because that's what's inside the orange.

And that's exactly how life works—when pressure is applied, what's inside you will come out.

So, from today onwards, fill yourself with positivity, peace and gratitude—because the world will always test you. When life squeezes you, make sure what comes out is strength, wisdom and resilience.

That's the secret to mastering your emotions and using the Law of Attraction to its fullest.

Are you ready to fill yourself with the right energy? Let's do it!

Day 91

The Tetris Effect—Why the Last Five Minutes of Your Day Matter

Let me ask you a question.

Have you ever played Tetris for a long period of time, and then, when you finally stop, you start seeing those falling blocks in your mind—while doing other things, even when you close your eyes?

Or maybe you've played a video game, and later, you see elements of that game in real life?

If you have, congratulations! You have experienced the Tetris Effect.

The **Tetris Effect** is a psychological phenomenon where, if you spend a lot of time on a particular activity, your brain begins to rewire itself to recognize patterns related to that activity—even outside of it.

This was first observed in people who played Tetris for long periods. Even after stopping, they reported seeing falling blocks in their dreams, in real life, and even while looking at buildings and objects. Their brains had been programmed to think in Tetris patterns.

But here's the most important part:

This effect is not limited to video games.

It applies to anything you focus on regularly—especially in the last few minutes before sleep.

We have already discussed how the subconscious mind is most receptive just before you sleep.

Science now proves this with the Tetris Effect.

Whatever you focus on right before you fall asleep—your brain absorbs, processes and reinforces while you sleep.

So, if you:

- Scroll through negative news or social media drama, your mind will reinforce stress and negativity.
- Worry about your problems, your subconscious will magnify them, making you wake up anxious.
- Replay past failures or arguments, your subconscious will strengthen that emotional distress.

On the other hand, if you:

- Visualize your goals, your brain will start working towards them while you sleep.
- Repeat affirmations, your subconscious will reinforce those beliefs, making them feel more real.
- Practise gratitude, your mind will wake up in a state of abundance.

This is why the last five minutes of your day are the most powerful.

Since your subconscious rewires itself based on your last thoughts before sleep, we can use this power consciously to manifest faster. See, video games can teach us good things too! The Tetris effect is a demonstration of repetition, but the question arises, how do we use this in our lives to impact them positively? Well, as usual, I am here to walk you through it.

Step 1: Set an intention before sleeping.

Before lying down, take a moment to decide what you want to reinforce in your mind overnight.

Do you want to:

- Attract more money?
- Improve your health?
- Manifest your life partner?
- Manifest a specific goal?
- Wake up feeling peaceful and positive?

Your last thought before sleep will set the tone for your subconscious processing.

Step 2: Visualize your dream life.

Close your eyes and see yourself already living your dream life. Feel the emotions—happiness, excitement, gratitude—as if it has already happened.

Step 3: Repeat positive affirmations.

Softly repeat affirmations aligned with your desires. For example:

- *I am financially abundant.*
- *I wake up happy and full of energy.*
- *Everything I desire is coming to me effortlessly.*

This will programme your subconscious to believe in these truths.

Step 4: Fall asleep with gratitude.

The easiest and most powerful thing to do before sleep is to simply thank the Universe for all the good things in your life.

Example: *Thank you for today. Thank you for my health, my opportunities, and all the good coming my way.*

Gratitude raises your vibration, and your subconscious will focus on abundance rather than lack.

The Tetris Effect proves that what you focus on before sleep stays with you.

So, if you want to change your reality, start by changing your bedtime routine.

Tonight, instead of worrying, overthinking, or watching negative content, take just five minutes to visualize, affirm and express gratitude. Do this consistently, and you will start noticing how your thoughts, energy and even your reality begin to shift.

Remember: Your subconscious is always working—make sure it's working in your favour!

So, what will you focus on tonight?

____

____

____

Day 92

The One Thing That Will Ruin Your Manifestation—Haste

You've been following the Law of Attraction for quite some time now. You've been visualizing, writing affirmations, practising gratitude and keeping your energy high.

But then, the thoughts creep in . . .

Why isn't it happening yet?

I've been manifesting for so long, but where is my result?

Maybe this isn't working . . .

And just like that, everything you have been working towards starts slipping away.

Why?

Because 'haste makes waste'.

There is a reason the saying has been passed down for generations. It teaches us that when we rush, we make mistakes. We miss details, lose patience and, worst of all, we create resistance.

The same applies to manifestation.

The moment you start feeling desperate for your manifestation to happen, you shift from positive expectation to negative frustration. And when your energy shifts to frustration, the Universe gets a signal that says:

'I don't have it yet. I'm not happy. I'm not trusting the process.'

Guess what happens next?

Instead of attracting what you want, you push it further away.

The Law of Attraction follows energy alignment. Whatever you think and feel, you attract.

- If you feel desperate → you attract more desperation.
- If you feel impatient → you attract more waiting.
- If you feel abundant and calm → you attract abundance and ease.

Now, let's bring back a lesson from Day 10: *Letting Go and Surrendering.*

Do you remember the Bhagavad Gita verse?

'कर्मण्येवाधिकारस्ते मा फलेषु कदाचन ।'

You have the right to perform your prescribed duty,
but you are not entitled to the fruits of your actions.

This means: Do your work, take the right actions, but don't obsess over the results.

Your job is to put in aligned effort. The Universe's job is to decide when and how your manifestation arrives.

If you've been feeling impatient about your manifestation, here's how to correct it:

1. *Shift from 'when will it happen?' to 'it is already happening'.*
   Instead of stressing over the timing, trust that the process has begun. The energy has already been set in motion.

2. *Stay busy in the present moment.*
   The best way to let go of impatience is to focus on something else.
   Work on new goals, hobbies and daily routines that make you happy.

3. *Visualize the end result, not the timeline.*
   Stop looking at the clock. Stop counting the days. Only focus on the feeling of already having what you desire.

4. *Use the 'I trust you, Universe' mantra.*
   Whenever you feel impatient, close your eyes and say: 'I trust the Universe's timing. Everything is happening at the perfect moment.'

5. *Think of past manifestations that came at the right time.*
   Hasn't life surprised you before?
   Haven't good things come to you exactly when you needed them?

Use this as proof that the Universe knows what it's doing.

You don't plant a seed today and expect a tree tomorrow.

You don't start a workout today and expect abs in twenty-four hours.

Similarly, you cannot force a manifestation to happen before its time.

Let go. Stay patient. Trust.

The Universe is never late. It is simply waiting for the perfect moment.

And when that moment comes, you will look back and realize that everything was always working in your favour.

Day 93

Recognizing God's Plan—How the Universe Sends You What You Desire

For the past ninety-two days, we have been working on manifesting our desires, visualizing our dreams and aligning ourselves with the energy of abundance. We know that if we practise the Law of Attraction the right way, the Universe, or God, will send us exactly what we ask for.

But here's a question that many people ask me:

'How will I recognize when God is actually giving me what I manifested?'

You see, God's plan is not always direct. The Universe does not always hand you what you desire in the exact way you imagined. Instead, it sends signals, people, opportunities and pathways that lead you to your manifestation.

But the real question is: *Are you paying attention?*

Imagine you place an order at a restaurant for apple juice. The waiter notes it down, and now, all you have to do is wait for it to arrive.

But what if the waiter doesn't bring it in a glass?

What if, instead, he brings you a fresh apple?

Would you refuse the apple just because it's not in the form you expected?

Or would you take it, knowing you can still make the juice?

This is exactly how God works. He always sends us what we ask for, but not always in the form we expect.

Here are three real-life ways God's plan could be working for you right now:

Example 1: The apple juice analogy

- Let's say you are manifesting apple juice.
- You expect a fresh glass of it, but instead, a friend brings you an apple.
- You might feel disappointed at first, but if you take a moment to think, you'll realize you can make apple juice from it.

Lesson: The Universe might not hand you your desires directly. Instead, it provides the resources, tools and opportunities for you to create them yourself.

Example 2: The dream job opportunity

- You want a higher-paying job with better benefits.
- You expect to receive an immediate interview call from your dream company. But instead,
- A long-lost friend reconnects with you and tells you about an opening in their company.

- Or maybe you stumble upon a job listing while randomly browsing online.

At first, it might not seem like your exact manifestation. But if you take action on the opportunity, it could lead you to the job of your dreams.

Lesson: The Universe creates a pathway for your desire—it's your job to recognize it and walk through the door.

Example 3: Meeting the love of your life in an unexpected way

- You have been manifesting a loving, supportive life partner.
- You expect to meet them randomly at a coffee shop or through a dating app. But instead,
- You bump into an old acquaintance, and they invite you to a gathering.
- At that gathering, you meet someone who turns out to be your perfect match.

If you had ignored the invitation or thought it was random, you would have missed your manifestation.

Lesson: God's plan works through connections, coincidences, and small decisions. Trust the process and follow the path he is showing you.

When we ask God or the Universe for something, we often expect it in a specific way. But the truth is, we cannot control how it comes to us.

- Maybe you want money, and instead of receiving a direct deposit, you suddenly find a new business opportunity.
- Maybe you want peace of mind, and instead of everything becoming easy, you are sent challenges that teach you patience and inner strength.
- Maybe you want love, and instead of instantly finding 'the one', you first go through self-growth to prepare yourself for the right person.

God's plan is always greater than your imagination. But to receive it, you must do three things:

1. **Recognize the signs.** Opportunities will come in unexpected ways. Pay attention.
2. **Take action when a door opens.** When the Universe presents a path, walk through it.
3. **Trust divine timing.** Just because it isn't happening the way you expected doesn't mean it isn't happening.

So, from now on, be open to the gifts that come your way, even if they don't look exactly like what you asked for.

Because God always delivers—but you must be ready to receive.

Day 94

The Universe is Like Google— Whatever You Search for, You See!

Today, we are having a fun yet eye-opening discussion about how the Law of Attraction works exactly like Google!

We often wonder, 'How does the Universe show us what we desire?' Well, think of it like this:

Whenever you want something, you 'search' for it by writing affirmations or thinking about it.

Just like Google, the Universe takes your request and starts showing you things related to it everywhere in your reality.

Sounds fun, right? Let's break it down with some simple (and hilarious) examples!

Let's say you suddenly decide you need a new tiffin box for your office lunches. You start thinking about it, wondering what colour or size you should get.

You write an affirmation:
Thank you, Universe, for my brand-new, stylish tiffin box!

Guess what happens next?

Suddenly, your colleagues start bringing their fancy tiffin boxes to work. You never noticed them before, but now they seem to be everywhere. Some might even show off their lunchboxes to you without you asking!

The Universe is just like Google—it picks up your 'search query' (your thought) and starts showing you related results.

Let's say you're feeling a little sick, and you Google: 'Best doctor near me.'

What happens next?

For the next several days, everywhere you go online—Instagram, Facebook, YouTube—you start seeing ads for hospitals, pharmacies, health supplements and medicine!

Google took your search and started throwing relevant content at you.

Now, replace 'Google' with 'The Universe'.

This is exactly how the Law of Attraction works!

Whatever you think about constantly, the Universe will show you more of it. If you focus on problems, you will see more problems. If you focus on solutions, you will start finding opportunities.

It's that simple!

Since we are comparing the Universe to Google, let's test it right now.

I want you to picture Aladdin's magical lamp in your mind. Close your eyes and visualize it for a few seconds.

Now, say this affirmation ten times with full intention and emotions:

Thank you, God! I just found the most beautiful-looking Aladdin's lamp for my display collection.

That's it! You have now placed your 'search request' into the Universe.

Here's what I want you to do:

1. Go about your daily life as usual. Don't actively search for Aladdin's lamp anywhere.
2. Over the next seven days, pay attention!

- Maybe you walk past a store and spot an Aladdin's lamp on display.
- Maybe you randomly scroll on social media and see a post about it.
- Maybe a friend unexpectedly brings up Aladdin in a conversation.
- Or maybe . . . you actually end up buying one!

3. Come back here and write down what happened. Use the space below to document your result:

- How many Aladdin's lamps did you spot this week?
- Did you end up buying one?

Write your experience here:

The Law of Attraction doesn't judge what you are searching for. It simply brings more of whatever you focus on.

So, from today onwards:

- Focus on positive desires, not fears.
- Search for solutions, not problems.
- Speak about what you want, not what you don't want.

Remember, the Universe is always listening—just like Google. So, what will you 'search' for next?

Day 95

Struggling to Visualize?
Try This Simple Remedy!

Have you ever felt frustrated because you just can't visualize your dreams properly?

You're not alone! A lot of people face this issue when they first start practising the Law of Attraction.

And today, I have a simple but powerful solution for you.

But before that, take a deep breath.

Relax your mind.

And let's have a conversation.

Visualization is like watching a movie in your mind, but some people say their screen is blank!

Does this sound familiar?

- 'I try to see my dream car, but I can't picture it clearly.'
- 'I want to visualize my success, but my thoughts keep distracting me.'
- 'I don't know if I am doing it right.'

This happens because your mind is too cluttered. When there is too much mental noise, you can't focus properly on creating a clear image.

That's where today's remedy comes in.

If you're struggling with visualization, do this simple meditation technique before you start.

Step 1: Sit comfortably

Find a quiet place. Sit in a relaxed posture—on a chair, a couch or even on the floor. Keep your spine straight but stay comfortable.

Step 2: Close your eyes

Gently close your eyes and bring your attention inward.

Step 3: Deep breathing

Take slow, deep breaths. Inhale through your nose for four seconds, hold for four seconds, and exhale through your mouth for four seconds. Do this a few times.

Step 4: The 'five sounds' technique

Now, focus on five different sounds around you.

- Maybe it's the hum of a fan.
- The sound of birds chirping outside.
- Someone cooking in the kitchen.

- The subtle tick of a clock.
- Even your own heartbeat.

For ten minutes, just listen and observe these sounds without judgement. Let your mind slow down.

This technique forces your brain to shut out distractions and become fully present.

By the time you finish, your mind is calm and clear, and visualization becomes much easier!

- Your imagination will feel sharper.
- Your focus will improve.
- Your affirmations will feel more real.

After doing this meditation, immediately start your visualization practice.

Imagine:

1. Your dream life is unfolding before you.
2. Your goals have been achieved.
3. Your future self is living in success and happiness.

Doesn't it feel more effortless now?

This simple practice removes mental fog and allows your subconscious mind to absorb the vision more powerfully.

If you've been struggling with visualization, don't give up! You just need to quiet your mind first.

From now on, before every visualization session:

- Meditate for ten minutes using the 'five sounds' technique.

- Then, immediately visualize.

This is your game-changer. Try it for the next seven days and see how your visualization transforms!

Your dreams are waiting for you; make them crystal clear.

Day 96

The One Fix That Will Speed Up Your Manifestations

Let's start with a question:

How many times has this happened to you?

You sit down to watch a movie, but then your phone vibrates.

Just one notification . . . You check it, then scroll through one reel, then another and another . . .

Before you know it, an hour has passed, and the movie you sat down to watch? You didn't even pay attention to it.

Or maybe this sounds familiar:

You're at work. Your body is at the desk, but your mind? It's already at home, thinking about your cosy bed and that nap you'll take later.

Here's another one:

You're sitting with your family at the dinner table, but instead of talking, everyone is glued to their phones.

This is the one flaw that keeps delaying your manifestations.

The Law of Attraction works best when your energy is fully in the NOW.

Think about it—if your mind is always somewhere else, your energy is scattered. And if your energy is scattered, your manifestations take longer.

Once I understood this, I made one major change in my life:

I started living in the present.

When you truly focus on the present moment:

- You give 100 per cent of your energy to what you're doing.
- You align with the vibration of your goals faster.
- You eliminate distractions that pull you away from your desires.
- You develop a sharper, clearer and more positive mindset.

And the best part?

The Universe sees this focused energy and rewards you quicker!

Here's the problem—if you constantly divide your focus, you're training your brain to be scattered and unfocused.

- If you're studying while listening to music, checking messages, and browsing the internet—how much of that study session do you actually remember?
- If you're exercising but your mind is occupied with office stress, are you truly working out efficiently?

- If you're eating while watching TV, scrolling on your phone or stressing about tomorrow—are you even enjoying your meal?

The truth is:
When your mind is divided, your results are delayed.
Starting right now, make this your new rule:

1. If you're studying, no music, no distractions.
2. If you're dancing, don't watch a movie while doing it. Feel the rhythm!
3. If you're working, stop thinking about your bed and focus on your work.
4. If you're eating, no TV or YouTube. Just enjoy your meal.

When you truly immerse yourself in every activity:

- You work better.
- You feel more satisfied and less stressed.
- Your productivity increases.
- You start manifesting your desires FASTER.

The Universe responds to focused, powerful energy.

If you can train your mind to stay present, to enjoy each moment without distractions, you will see a major shift in your manifestations.

So today, fix this one habit, and watch how quickly your life starts aligning with your dreams.

Day 97

Look Forward, Not Backward

Brain teaser: Where do you look while driving?

Imagine you're driving a car on a long, open road. Where do you focus your eyes?

On the road ahead, right?

Now, think about this: your car has a rearview mirror too. It's small compared to the windshield. Why is that?

Because while it's important to check what's behind you, your main focus should always be on where you are going.

That's exactly how life works.

Many of us get trapped in the cycle of regret, guilt, and overthinking. We replay past mistakes like a broken record:

I should have taken that opportunity . . .
I wish I hadn't wasted so much time . . .
If only I had made a different choice . . .

But here's the harsh truth: your past is like a road you've already driven through. You can't go back and change it.

What happens if a driver keeps looking at the rearview mirror instead of the road ahead?

They will crash.

The same happens in life when we dwell too much on our past. We slow down, we miss opportunities, and worst of all, we become stuck.

Let's go back to the car analogy.

A driver doesn't ignore the rearview mirror completely. They glance at it quickly to check what's behind, understand the situation, and adjust their driving accordingly.

That's exactly how we should treat our past.

Instead of carrying the weight of past regrets, we should simply take lessons from them and move forward.

- Did you make a mistake in your career? Learn what went wrong and make smarter decisions moving ahead.
- Did you lose an opportunity? Instead of regretting it, focus on creating new ones.
- Did you go through heartbreak? Take the lessons from that experience and use them to build better relationships in the future.

The past is only useful if we use it as a guide, not as an anchor.

If you want to drive your life at full speed towards your dreams, follow these simple rules:

1. Keep your eyes on the road ahead.

The future holds endless possibilities, but you'll never reach them if you keep staring at the past.

Start your day by setting goals, visualizing success, and focusing on what's next.

Ask yourself:

- *What do I want to achieve today?*
- *What small steps can I take towards my bigger goal?*
- *What am I doing right now that will help my future self?*

From now on:

Each morning, write down one thing you can do today that will bring you closer to your dreams. Then, do it.

2. Use the past as a mirror, not a chain.

Mistakes don't define you—they refine you.

Instead of beating yourself up over what went wrong, analyse it, learn from it and move forward with wisdom.

- A driver doesn't stop driving just because they see a car behind them in the mirror.
  Similarly, you don't need to stop moving forward because of your past.

Here is what you have to do!

Write down one mistake from your past. Instead of regretting it, list three lessons you learnt from it.
Now, apply those lessons to your present.

3. Shift your focus to possibilities, not regrets.

The Universe responds to where your energy is focused.
If you constantly think about:

- *Missed chances* → you will keep missing chances.
- *Past failures* → you will attract more failures.
- *Regretful moments* → you will feel stuck in them forever.

But if you start focusing on:

- *New opportunities* → more will come your way.
- *Lessons learnt* → you will grow and improve.
- *Future goals* → you will take action and manifest success.

So, each night before sleeping, write one positive thing that happened today. This keeps your mind focused on progress, not regret.
There's a reason why the windshield is bigger than the rearview mirror.
You are not meant to live in the past. You are meant to move forward.

So today, make a decision:

1. Stop looking back with regret.
2. Start looking forward with excitement.
3. Keep your eyes on the road ahead, and drive towards your dreams.

Your best days are not behind you; they are in front of you. Keep moving!

Day 98

Look Within—Your Positivity Is More Powerful Than Their Negativity

A common concern: 'How will the law of attraction work if no one around me believes in it?'

Many people ask me these questions:

- 'What if my family doesn't believe in the Law of Attraction?'
- 'What if my friends mock me for practising affirmations and visualization?'
- 'What if my environment is constantly negative?'

Here's my answer:

You do NOT need anyone else's belief for the Law of Attraction to work for YOU.

Your energy is yours alone; it is independent of the opinions, beliefs and doubts of others.

But what if I told you that instead of their negativity affecting you, your positivity can affect them?

If you're in a dark room, what happens when you light a small candle?

The darkness disappears.

The same is true for your positive energy. A single bright, positive person can outshine negativity in an entire household, workplace or friend group.

- You don't have to convince others to believe in the Law of Attraction.
- You don't have to explain why you practise gratitude or visualization.
- You don't have to get frustrated when others doubt you.

All you have to do is keep shining.

Over time, they will notice that you're:

- happier than before
- attracting success effortlessly
- handling problems with calmness
- moving forward in life with confidence.

And then, they may start wondering: *What is this person doing differently?*

That's how you lead by example.

Many people think that they need their family, friends or society to approve of their belief in the Law of Attraction.

But if you look at history, every great visionary was once doubted.

- **Wright Brothers:** People laughed at the idea of flying machines. Today, airplanes are a reality.
- **J.K. Rowling:** She was rejected by twelve publishers before Harry Potter became a global phenomenon.
- **Cristiano Ronaldo:** He was told he was too skinny to be a great footballer. He trained harder and became one of the best in the world.

What if these people had waited for approval before chasing their dreams?

You don't need anyone's permission to manifest the life you want.

If you are surrounded by doubt, criticism or negativity, follow these simple steps to protect your energy:

1. **Stop seeking approval.**

You don't need to prove anything to anyone. The Universe listens to your energy, not their doubts.

Affirm this: *I believe in my journey, and I trust the process.*

2. **Be the source of positivity.**

Instead of absorbing negativity, be the one radiating positivity.

- When people complain, try shifting the conversation towards solutions.
- When people spread negativity, stay neutral or walk away.

- When people doubt you, smile and keep believing in yourself.

Soon, your energy will influence them more than their negativity influences you.

3. Create a personal positivity zone.

If your surroundings feel negative, create a mental or physical space just for you.

Decorate a small corner of your home with things that uplift you—vision boards, motivational books, candles. Listen to uplifting music, podcasts or affirmations daily. Journal about gratitude, dreams and goals to keep your energy high.

4. Protect your energy like a shield.

Imagine a golden shield around you that blocks negativity but lets in light and positivity.

Whenever someone around you is negative, visualize this shield protecting your energy.

Many people have transformed their family atmosphere without forcing anyone to change.

1. A woman I know started practising gratitude by herself, even though her family was negative. Over time, she became calmer, happier and more successful. Eventually, her family naturally started adopting the same habits.
2. A man I coached visualized financial success daily. His wife initially mocked him, but when she saw his

consistent growth, she started manifesting her own goals too.

3. Another person kept focusing on personal growth, despite their toxic workplace. Instead of absorbing negativity, they stayed focused on their goals. Within months, they got a better job in a more positive environment.

You never need to force anyone to believe in the Law of Attraction. Your results will be proof enough.

If you're waiting for people to agree with your dreams, you'll be waiting forever.

Instead of looking at who doesn't believe in the Law of Attraction, start focusing on your belief, your positivity and your journey.

Because once you believe, the Universe will move mountains for you—no matter what others think.

So, stay strong, stay positive and keep manifesting. Your energy is all that matters!

Day 99

The Ultimate Brahmastra of Manifestation

Today is a special day—look at where we are! Did you ever imagine that these days would pass so quickly?

We are on Day 99, and today, I am going to give you one **Brahmastra** that will help you achieve exactly what you want.

We have been doing this for the past 98 days, but you might be wondering what is so unique about today.

Today, I will teach you how to get exactly what you want.

Remember when we talked about clarity? We discussed how it is important to be crystal clear when communicating with the Universe.

Well, today, I am going to give you one powerful secret that will help you refine your manifestation with laser-sharp precision.

The secret? Be precise about what you want!

Imagine you walk into a restaurant and tell the waiter, 'Bring me food.'

The waiter will be confused.

What kind of food? Chinese? Indian? Italian? Spicy or mild? What dish exactly?

Now, imagine you order with precision:

'I want a plate of hot, fresh butter naan with paneer tikka masala, mildly spicy, with a side of cucumber salad and a glass of chilled mango lassi.'

Guess what? You'll get exactly what you asked for.

The Universe works the same way. If you are vague about what you want, you will get vague results.

Let's break this down with real-life examples:

1. *I want to be rich.* → Too vague. What does *rich* mean?
   a. Do you want Rs 1 lakh per month or Rs 1 crore per month?
   b. Do you want wealth through business, salary, investments or passive income?
   c. What is the *exact* amount you wish to manifest?

Instead, say:

I am so happy and grateful now that I am earning Rs 10 lakh per month through my successful online business, and my net worth has crossed Rs 5 crore.

2. *I want to be successful.* → Success means different things to different people.
   a. For a rickshaw driver, success may be being able to pay his EMI and afford rent.
   b. For a corporate employee, success may be reaching the position of CEO.

   c. For a student, success may be securing admission to a top university.

Instead, say:

I am so happy and grateful now that I have become the top sales manager in my company, earning Rs 2 lakh per month, living in my dream home.

3. *I want the perfect partner.* → What does 'perfect' mean to you?
   a. Do you want someone adventurous, spiritual or financially stable?
   b. Do you want a loving, understanding and growth-oriented partner?
   c. Which values matter most to you in a relationship?

Instead, say:

I am so happy and grateful now that I am in a deeply loving relationship with my ideal partner, who is kind, understanding and shares my passion for travel and personal growth.

Think of the Universe as a genie. It grants you whatever you ask for, but the catch is that it follows exact instructions.

If you don't give clear instructions, you will receive something random, something that may not be exactly what you wanted.

The more specific and precise you are, the faster and more accurately the Universe can deliver your desires.

We are one day away from Day 100—the grand finale of this journey.

Here's what I want you to do today:

1. Take a piece of paper and write down one major thing you want to manifest.
2. Be as specific as possible. Mention exact amounts, dates and details.
3. Read it aloud and feel the excitement as if it has already happened.

This is your final Law of Attraction refinement before we conclude our 100-day journey.

Tomorrow is the last day, and it will be a special one. Be ready for it.

See you on Day 100.

Day 100

The Final Chapter—Your Manifestation Masterpiece

Take a deep breath. Close your eyes.

For the last 99 days, we have been on an extraordinary journey together. Today, on **Day 100**, we start as we always do—with gratitude.

As you sit comfortably in your usual spot, let's reflect on the path you have walked so far.

- Who were you 99 days ago?
- What were your thoughts, your doubts and your fears?
- What have you learnt? What have you gained?
- What has changed in you?

Think about the first time you read these pages—you may have been curious, sceptical or just looking for something different.

Now, look at yourself today—you are wiser, more aware and in control of your reality.

Do you remember the first time we spoke about affirmations?

The first time you did a visualization?

The first moment you realized that the Universe was responding to you?

Relive those moments. Smile at how far you've come.

Now, take another deep breath.

Are you ready for your final lesson? The final piece to complete your manifestation journey?

Let's begin.

We have spent the last 100 days together learning, growing and mastering the Law of Attraction.

We started with affirmations, learnt about visualization and discovered how our thoughts shape reality.

We practised gratitude, rewired our subconscious minds and even took bold actions towards our dreams.

We debunked myths, conquered fears and unlocked secrets that most people will never learn in a lifetime.

Somewhere along this journey, you felt the shift.

You started seeing signs. You noticed angel numbers, coincidences, and opportunities.

You realized your power.

The Law of Attraction works, and you are living proof of it.

But here's the catch—understanding it is one thing; mastering it is another.

And today, on our final day together, I want you to do something powerful . . .

Money is an energy exchange. What you believe, you receive.

Today, we are putting that belief into action.

Go to Google and search for:

'The Secret - Magic Cheque.'

You will find a printable cheque from *The Secret* book.

1. Print the cheque.
2. Write your name in the 'Pay To' section.
3. Write the amount of money you wish to manifest. Be specific!
4. Date the cheque for a future day when you expect to receive it.
5. Sign it under 'The Universe'.
6. Place it somewhere you will see it daily—on your vision board, wallet or mirror.

When you finally manifest this amount, return to this book and write below:

'I manifested my Magic Cheque on: ________________'

Imagine it's five years from today.

Everything you dreamed of has already come true.

You have achieved success, abundance, happiness and everything you ever wished for.

Now, from that future version of yourself, write a letter to the 'you' of today.

In the letter, tell yourself:

*   What your life looks like now.
*   How proud you are of your journey.

- The lessons you learnt along the way.
- How the Law of Attraction helped shape your destiny.

Write this letter with full belief, as if it has already happened.

Once you're done, hide this letter in this book. Forget about it.

One day, when you stumble upon it, you'll smile and realize . . .

Everything came true.

Now, let me leave you with the most important truth about manifestation.

The Law of Attraction is SIMPLE . . . but it is NOT EASY.

- Simplicity means anyone can understand it.
- Difficulty comes in consistent practice and belief.

Many people will read about the Law of Attraction.

Few will actually practise it.

Even fewer will master it.

The difference between those who succeed and those who don't is consistency.

This is where your real journey begins.

After 100 days, you now hold the ultimate power—the power to shape your reality.

You are the creator of your own life.

The more you believe, the more you receive.

So from today onwards, keep manifesting. Keep believing. Keep taking action.

Because with the power of the Law of Attraction . . .

You can manifest anything.
The journey never ends. This is just the beginning.

Congratulations! You are now a Master Manifester.

Notes

1   Bangert, M. 'Mapping Perception to Action in Piano Practice', Harvard Dash, https://dash.harvard.edu/bitstreams/7312037c-6324-6bd4-e053-0100007fdf3b/download, accessed on 5 November 2025.

2   'The Secret, Documentary', The Secret by Rhonda Byrne, YouTube, https://www.youtube.com/watch?v=_b1GKGWJbE8, accessed on 1 November 2025.

3   Byrne, Rhonda. *The Secret* (Atria Books, 2006).

4   Fredrickson, Barbara L. 'The broaden-and-build theory of positive emotions', *Philosophical Transactions of the Royal Society of London. Series B, Biological Sciences* (September 2004), pp. 1367–78.

5   Tello, Monique. 'A positive mindset can help your heart', Harvard Health Publishing (6 March 2019), https://www.health.harvard.edu/blog/a-positive-mindset-can-help-your-heart-2019021415999, accessed on 1 November 2025.

6   Steffens, Duane. 'Dr. Masaru Emoto: How Emotion Influences Water', BEZA Blogs, https://bornastheearth.com/dr-masaru-emoto/, accessed on 1 November 2025.

7   Murphy, Mark. 'Neuroscience Explains Why You Need to Write Down Your Goals If You Actually Want to Achieve Them', *Forbes* (15 April 2018), https://www.forbes.com/sites/markmurphy/2018/04/15/neuroscience-explains-why-you-need-

to-write-down-your-goals-if-you-actually-want-to-achieve-them/, accessed on 1 November 2025.

8   'Self-perception Theory', The Decision Lab, https://thedecisionlab.com/reference-guide/psychology/self-perception-theory, accessed on 1 November 2025.

9   '95 % Of The Day , You Are Not Operating From The Conscious Mind - Bruce Lipton', Success Archive, YouTube, https://www.youtube.com/watch?v=ZjZvtrKNvzU, accessed on 5 November 2025.

10   'Self-Affirmation Theory', EBSCO (2021) https://www.ebsco.com/research-starters/psychology/self-affirmation-theory, accessed on 1 November 2025.

11   Haefner, Joe. 'Mental Rehearsal & Visualization: The Secret to Improving Your Game Without Touching a Basketball!', Breakthrough Basketball, https://www.breakthroughbasketball.com/mental/visualization.html, accessed in 5 November 2025.

12   Weir, Kirsten. 'Forgiveness can improve mental and physical health', American Psychological Association (January 2017), https://www.apa.org/monitor/2017/01/ce-corner, accessed on 5 November 2025.

13   Ressler, Kerry J. 'Amygdala Activity, Fear, and Anxiety: Modulation by Stress', *Biological Psychiatry*, Vol. 67, No. 12 (15 June 2010), pp. 1117–19.

14   'Exercise can boost your memory and thinking skills', Harvard Health Publishing (26 August 2024), https://www.health.harvard.edu/mind-and-mood/exercise-can-boost-your-memory-and-thinking-skills, accessed on 5 November 2025.

15   de Sousa Fernandes, Matheus Santos, et al. 'Effects of Physical Exercise on Neuroplasticity and Brain Function: A Systematic Review in Human and Animal Studies', *Neural Plasticity* (14 December 2020).

16   'How simply moving benefits your mental health', Harvard Health Publishing (28 March 2016), https://www.health.harvard.edu/blog/how-simply-moving-benefits-your-mental-health-201603289350, accessed on 5 November 2025.

17 Vickers, Gay. 'The Power of the Words We Speak', Inward Bound Network, https://www.inwardboundnetwork.com/meditation-blog/power-of-words, accessed on 5 November 2025.

18 Salamon, Maureen. 'Gratitude enhances health, brings happiness—and may even lengthen lives', Harvard Health Publishing (11 September 2024), https://www.health.harvard.edu/blog/gratitude-enhances-health-brings-happiness-and-may-even-lengthen-lives-202409113071, accessed on 5 November 2025.

19 Lipton, Bruce. *The Biology of Belief: Unleashing the Power of Consciousness, Matter and Miracles* (Hay House India, 2015).

20 Shmerling, Robert H. 'The placebo effect: amazing and real', Harvard Medical Publishing (22 June 2020), https://www.health.harvard.edu/blog/the-placebo-effect-amazing-and-real-201511028544, accessed on 5 November 2025.

21 Salamon, Maureen. 'Gratitude enhances health, brings happiness—and may even lengthen lives'.

22 King, Vex. *Good Vibes, Good Life: How Self Love Is the Key to Unlocking Your Greatness* (Hay House India, 2019).

23 Steffens, Duane. 'Dr. Masaru Emoto: How Emotion Influences Water'.

24 Coreen, David. 'The Science Behind Goal Achievement', DAVRON (19 January 2024), https://www.davron.net/the-science-behind-goal-achievement/#:~:text=Dr.,who%20merely%20conceptualize%20their%20goals., accessed on 5 November 2025.

25 'From Louise Hay - The Power of the Mirror Work Technique', HealYourLife, YouTube, https://www.youtube.com/watch?v=BAgg1zY4aJo, accessed on 5 November 2025.

Scan QR code to access the
Penguin Random House India website